BETWEEN GOD AND SATAN

BETWEEN
GOD AND SATAN

HELMUT THIELICKE
**PROFESSOR OF SYSTEMATIC THEOLOGY
AT THE UNIVERSITY OF HAMBURG**

TRANSLATED BY

Reverend C. C. Barber, M.A., D.PHIL.

*Wm. B. Eerdmans Publishing Company
Grand Rapids, Michigan*

FIRST PUBLISHED UNDER THE TITLE OF 'ZWISCHEN GOTT UND SATAN'
BY FURCHE-VERLAG, HAMBURG, GERMANY

First Edition in English 1958
Reprinted, February 1960
Reprinted, November 1961
Reprinted, October 1962
Reprinted, August 1963
Reprinted, September 1969
Reprinted, August 1973

PUBLISHED IN GREAT BRITAIN BY OLIVER AND BOYD LTD.

LIBRARY OF CONGRESS CATALOG CARD NUMBER: 59-10213
ISBN 0-8028-1316-X

PHOTOLITHOPRINTED BY GRAND RAPIDS BOOK MANUFACTURERS, INC.
GRAND RAPIDS, MICHIGAN, UNITED STATES OF AMERICA

PREFACE TO THE THIRD GERMAN EDITION

THIS little book on the temptation of Jesus and the temptability of man appeared for the first time in 1938, and although it makes no direct reference to the religious and political conflict of the day it was intended to strengthen the followers of Jesus Christ in their resistance to ideological tyranny.

It was reissued in 1946, soon after the collapse of this tyranny. The temptations had indeed changed, but the tempter, the 'bringer into confusion', was the same, although he employed new threats and new allures. His strategic goal remained the same; only his tactical methods had altered. No one who has studied the temptations of Jesus can doubt the identity of the figure in the background despite the change of masks.

The author now issues his little book for a third time, in the confidence that in writing it he was not inspired solely by the compulsion of a particular day and hour—if that had been the case his words would have lost all meaning when that hour ended—but that it was written in obedience to the Lord, to whom all hours belong, and who therefore teaches his own to recognise in all of them the ultimate hour of the earth. It is that same hour in which we again and again are lost, and at the same time found. One who dares to hope that he has seen the hour of all hours and has raised his voice to indicate it, may at the same time cherish the hope that it may be proclaimed both before and after the catastrophe; not because he over-estimates the permanent value of his little piece of literature, but simply and solely because the same judgment and the same promises still hold good.

HELMUT THIELICKE

CONTENTS

PRELUDE

THE FIRST TEMPTATION

Then was Jesus led up of the Spirit into the wilderness to be tempted of the devil. And when he had fasted forty days and forty nights, he afterwards hungered. And the tempter came and said unto him, If thou art the Son of God, command that these stones become bread. But he answered and said, It is written, Man shall not live by bread alone, but by every word that proceedeth out of the mouth of God. Then the devil taketh him into the holy city; and he set him on the pinnacle of the temple, and saith unto him, If thou art the Son of God, cast thyself down: for it is written:

He shall give his angels charge concerning thee:
And on their hands they shall bear thee up,
Lest haply thou dash thy foot against a stone.

Jesus said unto him, Again it is written, Thou shalt not tempt the Lord thy God. Again, the devil taketh him unto an exceeding high mountain, and sheweth him all the kingdoms of the world and the glory of them; and he said unto him, All these things will I give thee, if thou wilt fall down and worship me. Then saith Jesus unto him, Get thee hence, Satan; for it is written, Thou shalt worship the Lord thy God, and him only shalt thou serve. Then the devil leaveth him, and behold, angels came and ministered unto him.

MATTHEW 4.1-11 (RV)

And all man's Babylons strive but to impart
The grandeurs of his Babylonian Heart.
                    FRANCIS THOMPSON: *The Heart*

Within his soul the ages meet in strife,
Small wonder demons haunt his daily life!
                    C. F. MEYER: *Hutten's Last Days*

PRELUDE:

BREAD, TEMPLE PINNACLES, AND SHINING LANDS IN THE DESERT SANDS

Then was Jesus led up of the Spirit into the wilderness to be tempted of the devil. And when he had fasted forty days and forty nights, he afterwards hungered . . .

1. *Vision in the Desert*

THESE words begin a story rich in colour and meaning. Against the background of the desert, mysterious, utterly isolated and infinitely remote, two figures are struggling for a huge stake. Are they gambling or are they involved in a relentless battle in this solitary place? And what is the stake?

We know the reason of the conflict. Here in the midst of the desert far from the world of men, these two are struggling for the earth and for man. And this earth is my world and yours. And this Man—is you and I. And those in conflict are God's Son and Satan.

An hour later the conflict is decided. Beaten, discredited and conquered, one of the two figures leaves the field. In a mysterious vision later Jesus sees Satan fall from heaven like lightning (Luke 10.18). The reflection of this lightning flashes on the horizon of the desert, when the devil flees. For he has indeed taken flight, and only for a season (John 12.31; Rev. 20.1, 2, 10) is he permitted to remain in exile and to make the world unsafe (Rev. 12.9; 20.7), that world whose secret prince he is (John 12.31; 14.30; 16.11), and in whose atmosphere (Eph. 2.2), in whose nights (Eph. 6.12; Col. 1.13) and days (2 Cor. 11.14) he hides, and out of which he torments the disciples with rearguard-actions (1 Tim. 4.1; 1 Peter 5.8), striving to make their hearts fail, and seeking whom he may devour.

And his opponent in the wilderness? Does he stride from this battlefield as we would expect: with head high and renewed might, crowned as the victor, and bearing a name which henceforth and visibly is to be set above every name (Phil. 2.9)?

By no means; how different is this victory from those of men! He rises to his feet, and immediately sets forth on his *via dolorosa*. He, too, goes forth into the world. Once again he will have to contend with the powers of evil which rise against him. He goes through this world, which is a theatre of war and a battlefield between God and Satan. By winning his first victory he has entered this world. Christ will fight for the souls of the men he meets, whether they be publicans or Pharisees, fools or wise men, rich youths or poor men, working-class men or lords of industry, the hungry and thirsty or well-fed and safe—he will fight for the souls of all these men alike, and he will die for all of them.

Thus does the victor in this fight take his way hence (Matt. 26.46), going straight towards his cross, as though God had forsaken him (Mark 15.34).

Is he not after all really the loser—a bankrupt king who has gambled away his crown—as he sets forth on his path from the desert to the cross? Has he not won a Pyrrhic victory? He travels the path beset with pain which leads to the cross, and not the way of glory and triumph which is also the way of God (for how can God's progress be other than triumphal?).

Perhaps this contest in the desert was after all a drawn game. Perhaps in the long run the dread opponent will prove to have won the victory and regained his power over the world. Is there any man alive in the twentieth century who does not think that all the evidence points in this direction?

But something more happens in the desert when the two go their ways: 'The angels came and ministered unto him' (Matt. 4.11). He must after all have won the victory.

2. *The Mystery of Temptation: Man as the god of God*

We begin to feel that our own fate depends on the outcome of this struggle between Christ and the devil. And so we will try to pay due heed to what is said to us in the wilderness and to what happens to us. For our destiny is at stake: Jesus Christ who is fighting here is not only 'the mirror of the divine heart' (Martin Luther), but also of the human heart (Phil. 2.7), a mirror of our nakedness and vulnerability and of our poverty and imprisoned state (Matt. 25.35ff). Jesus Christ's presence in the desert and his temptation hold a message for us: Look, through suffering and conflict the Son of God has become your human brother. For he bears the burden which oppresses you and which does more to shape your destiny than anything else in the world: Jesus suffers temptation with you. He shows you how life can be borne in its most critical and terrible hour—the hour of temptation. By himself confronting the Evil One, he shows you how to recognise this dangerous crisis in your life and where to seek salvation.

How can temptation be the determining factor—and the most deadly peril—of our lives? For temptation is a deadly peril. What other possible interpretation is there of the petition (Matt. 6.13): 'Lead us not into temptation'?

To be in temptation means to be constantly in the situation of wanting to be untrue to God. It means being constantly on the point of freeing ourselves from God. It means living constantly in doubt of God: 'How can I fulfil thy commandments, thou uncanny King? Let me go. Do not wise men collapse under this burden, as well as prophets and heroes? How can I change the thought in my heart (Matt. 5.28), thou dreadful searcher of this heart (Mark 2.8)? I am not even master of my actions and am powerless when they slip out of control! (Rom. 7.19). If thou wert God, thou couldst not command all this, thou couldst not make us black and then demand that we become white! Art thou then God at all? Are God's commandments really valid (Gen. 3.1)? Is not this dreadful law the fruit of evil fancies?'

Thus temptation gnaws at our hearts. It brings us almost to the point of freeing ourselves from God. We doubt his godhead and begin to remember that we are but human.

Or temptation attacks in a different way, and we say to ourselves: 'How can God send me this or that? Certainly I understand why he should send me illness. That was indeed wisdom, for I needed it. Did I not need a damper? Did I not need time for reflection? Did I not need to experience pain in order to mature, and to see the face of death, in order to understand life, through which I stormed in ignorance of its abysses and its limitations? Certainly, I stood in need of all this and must regard it as wisely sent. And because suffering, when regarded from this angle, seems to have meaning and purpose, it may, after all, come from a wise and conscious providence; it may come from—God.'

That is how I think about God. Aided by my intelligence, I make up my mind about him. I know how God 'must' act, in order to be really God. He 'must', for instance, be wise (wise in a way I can understand). He 'must' act in a way that makes sense and is best for me. He 'must' enrich my life with happiness and perhaps also with suffering (we clever human beings also know something about the uses of suffering!). He 'must' preserve our nation, for our nation knows it is called to a mission in the world, and that God and providence can only exist when this mission reaches fulfilment. God 'must' do all kinds of things if he is to be acclaimed as the true God. God 'must' turn stones into bread. He 'must' be able to leap from the pinnacle of the Temple, if he is to be acclaimed as God. It would appear, therefore, that it is we ourselves who set the conditions which God must satisfy in order that we may proclaim him God. We are God's masters.

In reality, exactly the opposite is true. The real truth—which sounds astonishingly simple when expressed 'theoretically'—is that, contrary to our illusions, God is our Master, and his thoughts are higher than our thoughts and his ways higher than our ways (Isa. 55.8f).

But although we are ready enough to concede this fact in theory, it looks very different when we meet it in everyday life, where our practice is diametrically opposed to our theory and we aspire to be the gods of God. And so we are immediately assailed by fresh doubts. For if we, who claim to be the measure of God, cannot understand his actions, we are tempted to ask: Did God really say this? Did God really do this? No—if God really existed he would act in a way more in keeping with his divinity!

3. *Job: The Torture and the Hourglass of the Tempter*

This doubt assails everyone who has to bear the suffering of which we have been speaking until it becomes so unendurable that it seems to us completely senseless.

The tempter struck Job with many plagues; he took away his goods, his servants, his children. He cast him down from the height of a full and pious life (oh! how easy it is to be pious when life is easy) into the horrors of naked and hungry poverty. 'The Lord gave, the Lord hath taken away; blessed be the

name of the Lord' (Job 1.21). Yes; with the last of his strength
Job grasps the meaning of what has befallen him; he hugs to
himself the word of God which he reads out of this misfortune
and clings to his consolation: 'It is God who speaks here; and
He can give and take away. But how could I ever have understood and respected his treatment of me if he had not also taken
away, and if he had not struck me down with a bitter blow?
In that case he would have remained a pious adornment of my
life and his service would have been an edifying cult in my rich
house, but only an adornment, the God in the Sunday niche.
Certainly, I would have lived honestly, and loved my neigh-
bours and my friends; I would have worked hard and kept on
good terms with him. But for all that he would never have
been the real lord of my life: he would never have been that
uncannily real Lord who can give and take away in ways past
finding out, and whose decisions are above our capacity for
understanding (Job 42.3). In no case would he have been for
me that Lord whose decisions I would have upheld unswerv-
ingly as right in all things and in all circumstances. No; he would
have been and remained a Lord with whom I would have dis-
puted and quarrelled and argued in my heart' (Job 42.4).

Job feels all this when God takes away his dearest possessions
and his loved ones. And he holds fast to this pious thought,
holds fast to it for a moment longer (even though doubt is
already beginning to raise its voice within him) when the tempter comes again and takes away not only his property and his
children, but even attempts his life and touches his bone and
his flesh (Job 2.5), when he touches the apple of his eye and
smites him with boils from the sole of his foot to the crown of
his head (Job 2.7).

So he sits in the ashes of his burnt goods and scrapes his
smarting, disfigured skin (Job 2.8), and clings fast once more
to the voice which resounds in all this: These evil and dreadful
things, too, we must receive at his hands, just as we receive
good things from him (Job 2.10). Or is it not goodness that we
should have to learn through pain that everything—everything,
pleasant and painful alike—comes to us at the hands and from
the heart of God?

But then the stark senselessness of it comes home to him; and
he can only think of the ashes and of his boils, his pitying friends

and burning pains. And in the background stands the tempter and measures with the hourglass, interested to discover when the limit of endurance—the human endurance of sufferings— is reached: the sand runs on; but first Job desires to attain a maturer knowledge of God; he thinks he perceives what God desires to say to him through all the pain he has brought upon him. But the tempter puts on a superior smile. He is going to win the bet. It is clear to him that two things will work in his favour: time and pain.

He knows that the wish to become maturer through suffering can only mean that the victim is prepared to let his sufferings be 'a lesson' to him, just as Job allows himself to be taught by the loss of his possessions that they belong not to him but to God and that God can take them from him, and that consequently God desires to reveal himself as Lord of life and death and property, when he intervenes so painfully in our lives.

The tempter laughs at this pious reaction. 'Yes', he thinks, 'we will wait for the moment when suffering has "taught" the good Job enough. That won't take very long. The pious maxims which he utters in his misfortune, and which will be rubbed in again and again, will no longer be heard when his suffering goes on.' Aye, indeed; 'when his suffering continues'. The tempter is a good psychologist; he calculates thus: Job thinks that when he has learnt enough from his suffering (e.g. that God gives and takes away and is the Lord) the suffering will cease, because it will then have fulfilled its function. For if it simply continued, he would not learn anything more and it would no longer have any 'purpose'.

And so the tempter, when he proposes to attack in earnest, allows the suffering to exceed the limits of what a man can regard as reasonable. The moment at which he thinks it must stop because he has learnt enough is precisely the moment at which it does not cease; it goes on senselessly. Time is the most uncanny minister of this prince of darkness. Time saps our resistance. Not because it goes on so long, but because it is so meaningless, and because suffering which goes on and on turns into a grotesquely scornful question: 'What do you say now?' 'Where is now thy God?' (Ps. 42.3). 'Do you still think this suffering is sent by God? What sense do you see in it? How can it still, after all these months and years, "be for your good"?'

'Are you really still holding on to your piety—and for how much longer?' 'Curse God and die' (Job 2.9).

Time is one method employed by the dark tempter. As time goes on, suffering appears more and more senseless and senselessness is the strongest argument against God. For what did we say? By our very nature, we and our intelligence (the proclaimer of sense) appoint ourselves the lords and judges of God. In time we cease to see any sense in his actions, let alone any higher purpose behind them. Therefore: Curse God and die!

The methods of the tempter are at once clumsy and subtle. At bottom he does nothing but play upon man's natural attitude to God and push it to its furthest extreme. He simply makes use of the qualities of human nature, for by nature man desires to be lord and judge of God. God's higher thoughts must always correspond—and even adapt themselves—to the thoughts of man, which man regards as having meaning. In this the tempter does nothing else but what we saw in Job: he leads man with the aid of time—i.e. with the aid of long-continued suffering—to a point at which man can no longer see any sense in his sufferings, and certainly cannot understand how they can give him maturity and help him on his way. This is the point at which, with diabolic inevitability, his belief in God appears absurd, and he abjures God.

The tempter sees his success with Job. He sees it with the many children of men; he sees it in long wars (how full were the churches at the beginning of the last war and how empty they were at its close!); he sees it in long, incurable, and horrible diseases; he sees it in a cruel, incomprehensible death. The tempter sees all these things, and happily, with a triumphant gesture, strokes the hourglass in which he has imprisoned time.

4. *The Doubter from the Beginning*

His other method is pain. We all know that from our own experience. Suffering is only educative as long as we are of unclouded mind and retain the power of thought—i.e. only as long as it serves us 'for reflection'. But this reflection ceases at once when purely physical pain passes a certain limit, the limit beyond which we are completely filled by it, and clench our teeth together convulsively or scream aloud, or wait—shaken

B

by fear and horror—in the hollow of painlessness (which lasts for a second) for the approach of a new wave of agonising pain. And every misfortune and every fight, whether in a theatre of war, or in the course of civilian life at home, or in a hospital or an asylum, is indeed such a pain if it brings us again and again to that limit at which we are 'completely filled', and lose even the power of questioning.

In such a situation, how can we possibly have edifying thoughts about sense or the lack of it, about the strength and maturity won through pain?

Yes, that is the tempter's other thesis: that there is a degree of suffering at which one ceases to mature. And this pain is the other arrow in the enemy's quiver: the pain which loses all meaning through its severity.

And therefore man, eager to bind God to him by his belief in God's purpose—i.e. by his belief in himself—dethrones this God of his, as soon as he himself becomes nothing more than a heap of writhing pain.

Thus man is a doubting and a tempted being from the start. That is bound up with his nature as a man. For he is a fallen and a separated being and no longer the friend of God. He is so no longer, though he does not for an instant admit it even to himself, and invokes God's name with the passionate fervour of Job, and although clouds of incense surround him like a mist which almost hides the flash of the cherub's sword barring him from the garden in which he once felt the nearness of God.

So he must needs be a doubter from the very beginning of his journey, as indeed, from his cradle onwards, every single human being must be. He is for ever Job whose belief in God is shattered; for God is not as he believed him to be. His creed was no more than a cunning system of keeping account of a divine 'justice', with a kind of moral world order which sees to it that it goes well with the pious and badly with the wicked. It was the belief that 'world-history is world-judgment' because a just God holds this world-history in his hand.

But God is not just in the accepted meaning of this belief which is now being tried and tested by being torn asunder. Yes, God is 'unjust'; he puts the pious Job, impoverished and disfigured, in a heap of ashes, where he scrapes his boils. And meanwhile villains prosper, and so do scoundrels and shirkers and thrusters, and the sun of God shines—with painful 'injustice'—on the good and on the evil (Matt. 5.45).

Yes, God is different from this belief; for this belief is belief in a purpose (e.g. in the purpose behind suffering) and God appears suddenly to have no purpose; we do not understand his ways and therefore we ask: Is God really there at all? Does God exist?

This belief is belief in the highest wisdom; and lo—God is foolishness (1 Cor. 1.18, 21).

This belief is belief in the glory of God and in his splendour; and lo—God comes near to us despised and spat on and nailed to the tree of torment.

This belief is belief in miracles (1 Cor. 1.22); and lo—God is silent (Matt. 12.39) and does not descend from the cross (Matt. 27.40).

This belief is belief in a greatness in and above the world (1 Cor. 1.22ff); and lo—God is small and is an occasion of stumbling (Isa. 8.14).

This belief storms forwards and seizes hold of God's robe; and lo—God comes quietly, noticed by no one, through the back door of the world, and lies in the stable of Bethlehem.

This belief is belief in the day; and lo—God comes by night, and is hidden from the wise and prudent (Matt. 11.25), but the Christmas shepherds—the 'foolish ones'—know him (Luke 2.7ff)—and the demons (Matt. 8.29) and children (Matt. 21.16).

This belief is always, secretly and under cover, a belief in man himself; and lo—God is God and not this human being. Therefore this human being and all of us are doubting and tempted beings from the start. For we know that God breaks us to pieces before he raises us up. God drives us with scourges out of the temple of our self-worship and smashes the Babylonian tower of our pride before he becomes our Father. God plunges us into a sea of uncertainty about ourselves and our aimless unrest, before he gives us peace.

And we do not want anything in common with this God. We want a cheaper peace. Therefore we take the wings of the morning and flee unto the uttermost parts of the sea (Ps. 139.9), flee into the drunken stupor of forgetting, in which we are no longer aware of the questioning, pursuing God, or of ourselves. We flee into the drunkenness of oblivion which we find in our work, or our daily round, or the anonymity of mass-existence, or alcohol, or sex, or the ceremonial of mass-life, in which, with fanatical enthusiasm, and surrounded by the noise of fanfares, we think we see the godhead above the stadium or the gigantic meeting-hall.

We are doubters from the beginning: we doubt God in the same measure as we believe in ourselves; and we have unbounded belief in ourselves. We believe for example in our immortality (Gen. 3.4), and that means presumably that we believe in our eternity and in the eternity of our race. And therefore we bite jubilantly into the forbidden fruit. Who can forbid us anything? Who has any right to say to us: 'Thus far, and no further!'? Has God that right? Are we not of his race, and do not earth and paradise belong to us?

We believe in our equality with God (Gen. 3.5) and therefore we say with the tempter, with the master of doubting, 'Hath God indeed spoken?' and we doubt God.

The hour of temptation is the hour in which we believe in ourselves, in which we cease to doubt ourselves, and therefore doubt God. That is our hour and the power of darkness (Luke 22.53). Thus does Holy Scripture teach of the breach of man with God.

5. *The Yearning to be free of God*

It is against the background of this biblical view of things that we must see the story of temptation.

Now we understand why man is tested and tempted from the beginning: because he believes in himself.

And we understand at last the meaning of the words 'man is in temptation'. He is constantly on the point of becoming unfaithful to God and making himself into God; he constantly desires to be free of God.

This wish to be free of God is the deepest yearning of man. It is greater than his yearning for God.

We are actually told that our rejection of God and our desire to be free of him is present in our piety, our yearning for God and even in the cunning use of God's own words. How the tempter in the wilderness streams with God's words! Why do the prophets thunder and preach against gods and idols, against cults and fetishes, and against the god 'Nature' and the god

'Fate'? Because all these are comfortable gods; because they are gods of rest and safety; because, being visible, no effort is needed to believe in them; because they affirm what man wants to have affirmed; they are nodding gods, and yes-sayers, and the originators of a pious intoxication which commits us to nothing, and of happy ecstasies. 'Great is Diana of the Ephesians!' (Acts 19.34); 'Hail to the other gods!'; 'Up for the dance round the golden calf!' (Exod. 32.1ff); 'O Baal hear us!' (1 Kings 18.26); 'Fate, come upon us!'

That is the immense monotone that runs through all the utterances of the people in the Bible: There is no greater yearning in man than to fall away, and for his own 'deep, deep eternity'. That they knew; for that the martyrs among them died. And this monotone resounds again out of the 'Crucify him, crucify him' (Mark 15.13) which merely plays like a short dramatically moving wave above a ground which remains eternally the same.

The mystery of the world is that it hangs thus between God and the Adversary and is always on the point of going over to the Adversary. That is the hour of temptation. It is the hour of Earth, the hour of this age. Therefore God has to die for this world and the cross marks the boundary between eternity and time. God and world stand 'crosswise' to each other. This is the truth, and the images and likenesses of the gods are lies.

But God is fighting for us all. It is completely incomprehensible, but it is the case: God loves us. We cannot conquer him, for we are only flesh and blood (Matt. 16.17; 1 Cor. 15.50); but he wrestles for us so sorely that the forehead of Jesus Christ is wet with sweat and blood (Luke 22.44).

But we should entirely misinterpret this fight of God for our souls (which the Bible proclaims to us) if we took it to mean that *we* are the fighters, wrestling, like Faust, for God—that we are the God-seekers (Jer. 17.5). We could not seek God at all, if he had not already found us; we could not love him, if he had not first loved us (1 John 4.10, 19).

No, we are not the heroes in this fight. We are the battlefield rather than the heroes or the army. The fight is for us, for we are fleeing. We live in the hour of temptation. We live in a world which has a lord (John 12.31; 2 Cor. 4.4). We live 'at the point of departure'.

It is into this depth that Jesus has come to us. It is here that the dayspring from on high has visited us (Luke 1.78). Here in the desert he has endured this bitter fate with us.

This completes the background. Now we turn our attention to the two figures in the foreground—Jesus and the tempter.

Jesus Christ came to us to suffer temptation, to suffer our fate with regard to God, and to become our brother. Let us go to him in the desert to see what he had to endure, and how he had to fight, so as thus to become our brother. Here we shall learn who we are and how it stands with this our world. The Bible always proceeds like this: how low we have fallen becomes clear to us in the effort God has had to make in order to help us. The theologians say: 'In the lowest depths it is made plain, not in the Law, but in the Gospel.'

The same thing happens here: who I am, who we human beings are, is made clear to us in the fact that Jesus must live through our life at its lowest point, that he has to be tempted in the same way as we are tempted (Heb. 4.15). Here, too, we learn who we are from the greatness of the effort which Jesus made and the suffering which he passed through for us by taking our place.

The desert is our world; the tempter is our tempter; the forty days and nights are our time, and we are Jesus, for here he stands in our stead. Who are we then, O God, who are we?

6. *Led by the Spirit into the Wilderness*

And Jesus was led into the wilderness by the spirit that he might be tempted of the devil.

We hear similar things of Moses; he was with the Lord forty days and forty nights and ate no bread and drank no water (Exod. 34.28). There he wrote the tables of the covenant. And amidst this solitude God spoke to him face to face, as a man speaks to his friend (Exod. 33.11). In this solitude something takes place on God's side. It is the hour of the nearness of God.

The man of God, Elijah (according to the Scripture), is also strengthened by God in his temptedness, his despair and emptiness, and goes forty days and forty nights, sustained by divine food, to the mount of God. The Lord appears there to this tired, worn-out, tempted man. And he has—contrary to expectation —not the form of a wild storm and the powers of nature in irruption; no, he appears in the surprising form of a still, small murmur of the wind (1 Kings 19.12). He is different, quite different from what the prophet hoped.

Like all the people of the Bible before him—and this is probably not unintentional, and is again the background of the event in the wilderness—Jesus, too, is now led into the stillness of the forty days and nights, to a tremendous encounter. But before he meets God, and before the angels come to minister to him, and before the joy of heaven shines upon him, he must first meet the 'Other One' and stand fast.

No other person has ever seen the 'Other One' thus, so dreadfully near, so unmistakably real—not Moses nor Elijah nor any man. And yet he stands behind us all, and is the secret prince of this world. But precisely because he is thus the prince of our world, we ourselves stand here with Jesus in the desert, and know that our own fate is at stake.

It seems to me very important that the tempter meets the Lord in the solitude of the desert. It is an unimaginable solitude, and not only are human beings absent—companions, parents, friends and strangers. Things too are absent; no traffic flows round him; no landscape holds his attention; there is nothing which he can inspect with interest; he cannot work; there is no entertainment for him. There is nothing at all, not even food and drink. Only the sand and the desert are round him.

And it is precisely here that he is tempted, where he cannot be distracted, led astray, or fascinated by anything. Could the tempter not have seized upon a more favourable moment? Why did he not choose the hour when the people desired to make him king (John 6.15)? Or when he hung on the cross and had the opportunity to descend (Mark 15.32)? Or when he stood before Pilate and knew, in the moment of extremest stress, that he could call more than twelve legions of angels to the rescue (Matt. 26.53)? Were not those hours of greater temptability? Were there not here stimuli, exciting chances, and fascinating glimpses into dreamlike possibilities? And yet the tempter comes here in the wilderness, into the greatest of all solitudes, in an hour which does *not* lie, like the others, at the dangerous zenith of life.

It seems to me that precisely this solitude needs to be medi-

tated on. In it appears the mystery of temptation. It is not
merely a painted scene, a theatrical background created by the
biblical narrator. No, 'the Holy Ghost *leads* Jesus into the
wilderness'. We must meditate on what this solitude may mean.
How should the Spirit of God do something 'without meaning'?

7. *The Babylonian Heart*

What goes on in us when we are tempted?

We can best make this clear to ourselves by quite simple and
ordinary forms of temptation, as for instance by the fact that
we are tempted to lie, to steal, to be vain, to be pretentious, or
to commit adultery. First—it seems—there is always an opportunity which attracts and entices us, which 'tempts' us. 'Opportunity makes thieves' says folk-wisdom, tersely and correctly.
The Bible tells us the same by throwing a sharply penetrating
light on the temptation of Adam and Eve. There is an un-
usually marked opportunity for sinning there; for in the midst
of the garden stands a tree of whose fruits one may not eat
(Gen. 2.17; 3.3). It is beset with the dangerous lure of mystery.
And its mystery is a continual alluring call to the eternal and
untamable urge in man to uncover every mystery. It is a call
to that curiosity which inspires science and technology, which
conquers the earth (Gen. 1.26), and in its deepest depths strives
to disturb and 'clear up' the mystery of the Most High.

Nevertheless it was not the apple, with its alluring mystery,
that 'was guilty' of the Fall. Who else was guilty of it but Adam
and Eve themselves? Man and not the apple was dangerous
in that paradisal hour. His avid desire to be like God, his
measureless hunger for equality with God, which was not con-
tent with mere likeness, and with being formed 'in the image
of God', brought catastrophe.

The serpent was not dangerous, nor was the apple; there was
no danger at all from outside; he himself was his own danger.
His Promethean heart that exploded was the charge of dynamite. That which comes 'from without' does not make man
unclean; it does not touch him, or touches him at most like a
tangent, and somehow does not belong to him (Matt. 15.11ff).
But what flows *out* of his heart, out of himself, can cause him to
die and depart from grace. 'For out of the heart come evil

thoughts, murder, adultery, fornication, thefts, false witness, blasphemy' (Matt. 15.19).

Then the serpent and the apple have only a little piece of work to do; the apple has nothing to do but smile a little at this over-full, thrusting heart, and let its own bright charms sway to and fro in the morning breeze, in order to be a last and ultimate cause of stumbling for this heart, already ripe for its wanton theft.

And the serpent has only to drop a little poison into his heart and so start a chemical process by which the image of this heart becomes visible and clear, just as the image on a photographic plate develops, although it was 'there' before.

Here we see the secret of temptation; the tempter is already enthroned in our hearts and rouses us to murder and theft (Mark 7.21-3). And the opportunity, which makes thieves, and every other external element, are mere auxiliaries and re-inforcing manoeuvres for his power—but not this power itself.

This we experience again and again in ourselves; when for the sake of our professional career we are tempted to deny a conviction; when we lie, or become dumb dogs when we ought to speak; when we are tempted to remove or to wish removed from our path one who is more able than we; when we 'look upon a woman to lust after her', when all this rises up in our hearts, to become in the next moment a horrible deed, crime, or mean action—then perhaps we succeed, in defiance (yes, in defiance!) of our impulse, in dominating the greed and mastering the temptation. Then perhaps we tame ourselves and perform, instead of the evil deed already crouching for the leap, what the traditional language of the Church calls 'a good work'. And so it may happen that from all this something is produced, i.e. a 'work', in which we cannot perceive the struggle, the temptation, and the horrible abyss over which it hung, and into which it nearly plunged.

But who could boast of these 'works'? Who of all those who stand in face of the law of God, and that means before his eyes, could ever forget that in them lay hidden this potential capacity for abysmal evil—this feverish readiness, as of a mysterious beast crouching ready to spring, and raising its head in fearsome fashion; who could forget that he was a murderer, in being angry with his brother (Matt. 5.21ff); that he was an adulterer,

in that he looked upon a woman to lust after her (Matt. 5.27ff);
that he swore falsely in that he said more than yea, yea, or nay,
nay (Matt. 5.33ff)? The secret of temptation lies within ourselves, in the thoughts of our hearts. It lies in the fact that we
are 'temptable'.

8. *The Moral Sortie out of Babylon*

This alone is the reason why so-called good works cannot
help us. Perhaps it really is the case that with the help of these
good works we overcame our temptation; perhaps we really do
help a poor epileptic, when we would rather have hated and
despised him for his repulsive fits and his impaired intellectual
condition. Perhaps we do pull ourselves up at the last moment
and remind ourselves that it is Christ who meets us even in this
beggar's garb, and that his painful cross is erected over this
poor life also. Perhaps we do help him now, lay a hand on his
head and speak kindly to him. But have we, in so doing, overcome the temptation itself? Have we filled up the abyss which
we saw yawning within our heart in the moment of temptation,
when we were ready for murder and lying and euthanasia?
Woe to him who thinks thus! It would be a deceitful and
prideful illusion to think that this 'good work' killed temptation,
that it could justify us, and that we might boast before him who
knows the heart, and whom not one of the surgings or beats of
this heart escapes (1 Cor. 1.29; 2 Cor. 9.4; Eph. 2.9). This man
should be told that his good work, with all its dazzling goodness,
is, among other things, just a camouflage for his heart; that he
hides his evil heart from himself and others—and from God
himself—by means of good works. But inwardly he is full of all
defilement, full of hypocrisy and evil-doing (Matt. 23.27f).
That is the curse of those who wish to justify themselves by
works. They overcome temptation with the great bravery of
Pharisees—and yet remain tempted, remain men in whom the
abyss yawns and the wound bleeds and the chain with which
they are fettered rattles. No man can leap over his own shadow.
Here the secret of temptation becomes quite plain; it is not
thrown into us from without by apples and serpents and 'opportunities', as a torch is thrown into a temple; no, we ourselves are
the tempted, and are always in temptation, even before the
opportunity arises.

9. *The Mirage of the Heart*

For this reason we cannot run away from temptation, but can only pray that God will not lead us into temptation; for we cannot flee from it by fleeing into 'good works', in order to put ourselves right with God by such 'works of the Law' (Rom. 3.20, 28; Gal. 2.16), and so clear our account with him. That is impossible, because wherever and however far we flee, we take ourselves with us—we remain the tempted, those who are on the point of deserting, the unprotected frontier.

And as a result we cannot flee from temptation by fleeing opportunities for sin; it is of no use to forsake the so sinfully fair world in the foolish belief that the world with its temptations is out there, and not rather within us, in our own Babylonian heart:

> And all man's Babylons strive but to impart
> The grandeurs of his Babylonian heart.

It is of no use to flee from the world so that this world of temptation does not cause a disturbance in our breast, in that remote cloister, which we are pleased to regard as the rock of refuge on that flight.

No, there is no solitude and no desert into which we can flee to escape temptation; the world is where we are, and our heart is nothing else but the microcosm of this world. Therefore the lusting and the tempting and the attracting and the alluring always go with us (Gal. 5.17; Jas. 1.14).

It is good to be clear about this. For only thus do we realise that in all stories of temptation *you* and *I* are the theme, not the wicked world *outside* or the 'evil scoundrels' (Prov. 1.10), or the serpents and apples. No, it means you and me when there is talk of temptation; it is our corporeal flesh that lusts against the Spirit (Gal. 5.17). It is our 'right eye' that offends us, and our hand that tempts us (Matt. 5.29f).

The point I wish to emphasise here is that this is the great implication of the fact that Jesus is solitary and apart, that he had to go into the desert to be tempted.

Here in the desert is the unmistakably solitary confrontation of God's Son with the tempter. Here all misunderstandings are excluded; there is no question of temptation being something external and accidental, as if it were a bit of the world and a bit of besotting tinsel. Where could there be found in all the sand, in all the silent endlessness, something which could entice and infatuate the Son of Man?

No, misunderstandings of that kind are here impossible.

10. *The Horror of Solitude*

It is the man in him that is tempted here 'like unto us' (Heb. 4.15). It is the man who is hungry and sees mountains of bread which would still his anguish; but where would there be real bread in this desert which might lead him astray? It is the man in him who sees the pinnacle of the Temple and a fantastic prospect opened to his ambition; but how in this desert could the real Temple be seen whose pinnacle might have led him astray? No, lurking ambition, the thought in his own heart, produces that image; the way of temptation goes from within outwards, not *vice versa*, and the Temple is a projection. It is the human being in him that hungers and thirsts to be a Lord and God of this world; already he stands on a high mountain and sees the glorious land and hears the promise that all this shall belong to him, if . . . But where is there in this desert a real mountain from which he could look down, and where in this desolate wilderness are those shining lands to be seen? No, here the lurking, crouching, tigerish hunger for an infinite kingdom, for boundless power and stupefying splendour, the secret thought of the heart, still in process of being conceived and not yet definitely formulated, paints the picture of incredible possibilities—a mad mirage of the heart.

Yes, the human being in him feels desire and is tempted. The man in him lusts, amid the joyless environment. Therefore all misunderstandings are here excluded. Therefore it is clear where temptation lies; it does not lurk without, but is within; it is not in front of us and has no open visor, but comes from behind and stands at our back. It is not some external Satan who stands between God and us; we ourselves stand between God and us, since the evil one 'possessed' us, just as the man in Christ stands here between him and God.

And do not we human beings know this only too well ourselves? Did not the rich young man know it, too (Mark 10.17ff)? In the last resort it was not his riches but he himself that stood between God and him; for he allowed himself to be possessed by riches. It was he himself who could not possess riches, as though he did not possess them (1 Cor. 7.30), and who was frightened to death when he was told to sell all that he had. Not his riches, but his having sold himself to riches was the weak spot (Matt. 6.24). Thus, too, Mammon is not the real wall which divides God and us, but we ourselves are that fiery zone in which we are possessed by those false lords—slaves who have sold ourselves and are enslaved by the urge to be emperor and king and God. It is not the Tower of Babel that divides us from God: that is only a parable, a parable of our will to be separated from God, projected into the external world. It is this will which builds the tower.

11. *The Vulnerable Point*

Only the fact that we ourselves are the tempted and the wounded can explain why we all (and particularly we modern folk) have such a vast fear of being alone. We know that we stand here confronted by ourselves. We must look into our own eye, and is there anyone we fear more than ourselves? It is no longer possible to push away all the decisive elements in our lives and all that puts guilt on us. We say: 'The woman thou gavest me . . . ' She did this thing (Gen. 3.12). No, it was you yourself. 'The serpent beguiled me and I did eat' (Gen. 3.13). No, you beguiled yourself. 'The Fate in my breast or the cosmic-ally determined Fate out there did it', thus the tragedians cry. No, it was you, and you alone. 'It was the character that thou gavest me.' (Here 'character' is to be understood always as something existing outside me, something detachable from me, something which overpowered me)—thus cries the accused, pleading diminished responsibility, mitigating circumstances.

Therefore the unredeemed man fears solitude, because there is nothing that he can appeal to here; he is confronted with him-self as with a kind of mysterious 'double', and there is nothing else but a great silence. Yes, he can only enter this solitude holding a cross in front of him, just as medieval man warded off the demonic powers with the crucifix.

This is the mystery of solitude, that here man stands at the point of his fatal temptation and gazes at himself out of a thousand mirrors, like one imprisoned in a 'Hall of Mirrors'.

It is for this reason that the student flees from his 'digs', and turns into the anonymous stroller of the High Street, and creeps away into cafés; he is afraid of himself.

It is for this reason that the week-end tourist, travelling by himself, takes his portable radio with him; the little box gives him the illusion that he is not alone.

It is for this reason that we—particularly we Christians, the more tempted we are—flee into our work, into the stupefying turmoil, into pleasure and lust, but at any rate into something. And has this flight not already become part of a programme in our public life, throughout this century and in all civilised lands? Isn't everything organised, even our freedom? Is there not everywhere a crowd waiting, into which we can plunge intoxicated, enraptured, orgiastic, raving, self-forgetting, abandoning everything, in a fashion only possible in the crowd, which carries one and lets one sink like an immense wave, and so makes one happy—immeasurably happy?

And is this twentieth century style of life not a dreadful token that we have lost grace—that we do not dare to be alone, but flee from the face of God, that might fall upon us and seize hold upon our identity? Thus we flee into the motley turmoil, flee into the onrushing programme of our work-days and holidays, flee into everything into which we can sink, with which we can excuse and 'justify' ourselves, just as Adam did: Look—the spirit of the age to which I was subjected; look at the crowd in whose flow I drifted with no will of my own, . . . look, look, look, . . .

That is the point: we cannot endure solitude because our relation to God is out of order. In the hour of solitude it becomes clear that there is nothing between heaven and earth to which we could appeal. And therefore we do not let this last solitude, in which Jesus stands here in our stead, ever break upon us, but prevent this by all means in our power. We never allow it to reach this point, just as we never allow ourselves to come face to face with God the Creator, but always fly to the non-dangerous gods, exchanging the glory of the immortal God for images resembling mortal men or birds or animals or reptiles (Rom. 1.18ff). But at bottom and secretly man knows—in the company of these his gods—that there is a God who has known us (1 Cor. 13.12) and who is a consuming fire; man knows this even when he actively avoids exposing himself to God. And at bottom and secretly he knows, too, how perilous is this last solitude, this confronting of oneself alone and being handed over to God naked and alone, even though by nature we never expose ourselves to that solitude, but prudently and timidly stay in the company of others.

Does not the deepest mystery of the fear of death lie here too? The decisive characteristic of death is the fact that it brings the hour of greatest solitude. Men and things are left behind. King and beggar, rich man and Lazarus are quite alone. It is like falling off a ladder. We grasp at a rung, but suddenly find that all the rungs have gone, and we grasp at the empty air. There is no cheque-book which we could flourish in the face of our creditors. And the crowd into which we plunged remains behind, beyond our reach. And the spirit of the age (how it carried us along, and how little we knew where we ended and it began!), the spirit of the age broods over waters from which we have long, long ago departed, and which now carry us no longer. That is the profoundest solitude, and therefore do we fear death. For now God will have us, even if we have him not. And for that reason even poetry veils this death and hedges it about with conciliatory illusions, and dreams of a transition to another form of this life, with new hiding-places and battle-fields and barricades, new crowds and spirits and intoxicating cups.

12. *Jesus our Fate*

Thus, then, we fear solitude and death, because there we are faced with the hour when we are alone with our guilt and are called upon to pass judgment on ourselves. And therefore death and solitude can only be borne—without illusions—if the grace of God supports our life and he is our Saviour who has trodden death and hell and all their powers beneath his feet. Only thus can we go into the wilderness; only thus can we confront ourselves, as the Son of God does here: by letting the Word fight for us (Matt. 4.7, 10) and not our flesh and blood (Matt. 16.17); and that means, in the last resort, by letting God fight for us, because we may have him for our friend and be at peace with him. Death, where is thy sting (1 Cor. 15.55)? God is here, Christ is here (Rom. 8.33ff).

Thus we understand why Christ was led by the Spirit into

the wilderness to suffer temptation as we do. We fear solitude, which is always solitude before the eyes of God, for here the truth of our lives bursts open unrestrained. It is this bursting open of human abysses (and that means of the abysses between God and man) that Christ endures here in our stead.

Jesus lives out our life in its most mysterious part, in its solitude, before us, as our example. Therefore there is now not one point in our life, not even the most diabolical or most tediously ordinary, at which we could still be lonely if we have Jesus for our Lord. He is our brother in temptation and solitude, he is man 'like unto us'; he has brought God down into this solitude, and has defeated the tempter. He is brother and Lord. Therefore we will go with him into the wilderness and pass with him through the stages of his temptation and his deathly solitude, as pious pilgrims kneel at the stations of his passion.

THE FIRST TEMPTATION:
THE REALITY OF HUNGER

And the devil said to him, If thou art the Son of God, command this stone that it may become bread.

13. *The Place of Temptation: The Realm of Concrete Things*

IN this question of the tempter's there are two characteristic features.

Firstly: The temptation of the Lord does not arise from speculations, nor, as we might say today, from contradictions, absurdities, or paradoxes in the concept of God. What tears and torments him is not the question of how it makes sense that God on the one hand is exalted above man in incomprehensible omnipotence ('What is man that thou art mindful of him . . . ?' (Ps. 8.4)) and that, on the other hand, he looks down into the hidden depths of man (Matt. 6.4), that insignificant speck in his immense world, and takes him to himself. These absurdities and contradictions do not tempt him. And yet it is precisely he, it seems, who is a living, crying witness to these absurdities and to many other contradictions, e.g. to precisely that contradiction between God's more than this-worldly majesty and his paternally consoling nearness. Are not all these incompatible things present in him: judgment and mercy, God and man, the Last Day and the stable in Bethlehem? Is not Christ a walking problem, the clash of conflicting and mutually jarring thoughts? Must he not on that account also be the living, moving object of all doubts?

But that seems not to be so: the temptation of Jesus does not originate in thoughts and speculations about God and himself; it does not originate in the mind at all; the temptation of Jesus has its origin in a completely matter-of-fact, nay, a crudely physical circumstance: hunger. He has fasted forty days and nights and is now hungry. And at this extremely well-chosen and obvious moment the tempter endeavours to upset his communion with God.

C   23

This is important. For in truth our communion with God is never called into question because this or that doctrine has caused us rational difficulties, because we could not imagine how Christ became man, or because the mercy and the stern judgments of God seemed intellectually irreconcilable. There are certainly plenty of difficulties like these, and they are oppressive. But something else is equally certain: that these intellectual difficulties are never responsible for creating the breach with God, the state of temptation. When they do appear, however, it is always a sign that something more concrete is not in order, namely our communion with God, our life in his sight. And after we have thus got out of order with God and have cut off our life from him—when all this has happened—we look round for reasons—and these present themselves swiftly enough.

In the first chapter of the Epistle to the Romans we are told how the heathen believe they see God in the four-footed, creeping, and flying creatures. One could say that Paul means nothing else here but that the heathen have become unfaithful to the one Lord, who is not to be pinned fast by any image or likeness, and that they have thus (as we put it) 'succumbed to the temptation' of unfaith and idolatry. But if one were to talk to these heathen, they would certainly know how to defend their idols and myths with many good reasons. With good reasons they would expound why they had gone wrong about God the creator (that creator proclaimed in the Bible), why their faith in him had been shaken, and for what reasons they had now sought refuge with gods and idols and philosophies.

14. The Wish as Father to the Thought about God

And yet all those reasons, which are as readily available as cheap market goods, would not be the real reason for the temptation of the heathen and the lapse of natural man into the worship of gods and idols: the real and fundamental reason never lies in the reasons and considerations supplied by intellect (which would perhaps be too myopic, too weak intellectually, to perceive God in his creation). The reason for the temptation lies rather in the whole attitude of men towards God, lies in the fact that man persists, obstinately and wickedly, in refusing to praise God and thank him, and show him in this way the honour due to him (Rom. 1.21).

The true cause of the temptation of the heathen is thus a very definitely concrete fact: their disturbed relation to God. This definitely concrete fact now gives shape (but after the event!) to their reasons, to their false knowledge of God, to their images and religions, to the clouds of their incense. The definitely concrete fact that they do not acknowledge God determines their knowledge of God. And the fact that they do not want to admit his existence later gives them, in plenty, the means of legitimising their desire. If the wish is ever father to the thought it is abundantly so here; especially, and in a terrifying way, it is father to our thoughts about God. How cheaply are thoughts and reasons to be had; how much more real and powerful is life itself and those wishes of ours, which produce, as if by magic, our thoughts and reasons—as plentifully and as opportunely as we could desire! The history of philosophy might well be written as the history of wishes; and the history of history-writing as a history of wishful thinking; and, indeed, the history of religions as a history of pious wishes.

The decisive factor to be noted here is that doubt and temptation never arise out of reasons or intellectual doubts; entirely on the contrary, doubt and the reasons for the doubt arise out of temptation which has already preceded them, out of the wound which has always already been received. And therefore we have to pray God that he search us and let us perceive what we mean (Ps. 139.23). For we do not know what we mean. We do not even know our own heart. We perceive and know only our reasons, and they are but a shadow of the real facts; they are, so to speak, only their ideological superstructure. 'Our reasoning springs from our convictions; our convictions are not the result of our reasoning', says Kierkegaard. Not only of the politician may it be said, but of every one of us, that in our speech and reasoning we conceal more than we reveal.

The art of political and tactical speech in general—alike for the man in the street and for the official spokesman—invariably consists in seeking reasons for our actions which we can make public, and thus keep to ourselves the true aims of these actions.

Similarly the art of diplomacy, like those of pastoral care or psychiatry in their different ways, always consists in seeing

through the reasons, looking into the heart and thus perceiving
the real life which puts forward these reasons. This true life
can only be found by going behind the reasons, for this life is
the concrete reality which produces them. As we really are, so is
our God (Luther's *Lecture on Romans*); and therefore, as we are,
so are the reasons with which we defend our gods, with which
we cast doubt on God the Lord—and these are likewise the
reasons with which the tempter does his work.

15. *The Shadow-Art of Apologetics*

This is fundamentally important. The man who is in the
fire of temptation, in the fiery furnace of trial, is as a rule also
in an inner cross-fire of argument, i.e. of reasons for and against
God, for and against Christ. But it would be foolish in this
distress to rely for help upon further reasons and telling counter-
arguments. This hollow art of counter-reasons and counter-
arguments, which is supposed to bring help against temptation
and to protect us from going wrong, is called apologetics. Apologetics claims to be the science of defending faith, and even of
warding off temptation. As if faith were something that could
be defended by us—and not rather something which is always
on the offensive and, far from giving ready-made answers
to the doubtful questions of men, turns the tables by putting
questions on its own account—aggressive, violent, radical questions—and striking straight to the hearts of men.

No; to try to drive out temptation with counter-arguments
and counter-reasons with discussion and apologetics is like
trying to chase away shadows with a shadow. In temptation
something much deeper is at stake. In temptation our whole
life is secretly loosed from God; we do not *want* his grace and
dominion, and all this becomes completely and bodily obvious
in our life, in its rush and dissatisfaction, in its lovelessness and
faithlessness, and above all in the endless shouting and talking
with which we drown the sound of all this, in our desire to
deceive ourselves and others. That is the very nature of temptation. The fundamental reality of our life, our communion
with God, is out of order. And this fearful state of not being at
peace with him, from whose love we cannot get free, looks for
reasons to justify itself. Temptation looks for arguments against
God—like coast-dwellers who hurriedly erect a dam against the

sea as it breaks in. And the reasons and arguments arise out of temptation like poisonous vapours out of a marsh. 'Reformed' theology has always known and proclaimed that rationality and its reasons do not say anything that is new in principle, but always merely express and clothe in words and thought-symbols what man really is. The tempted man thinks tempting thoughts. But in this the chief thing is the fact of being tempted. The real crux of the matter is solely and wholly this acute or chronic crisis of our communion with God. The thoughts, reasons and arguments which appear in the process are, in face of this reality, nothing but the delirious fancies of a sick man; they are only a symptom of the real illness.

At this point it becomes clear why we cannot fight temptation with thoughts, with apologetics. This would be tantamount to trying to drive out vapours with vapours, to drive out the devil with Beelzebub. No; here we are dealing with a swamp which must be cleared, an extremely real disturbance of a mighty reality—our communion with God—the cause of which must be removed. What we need is not thoughts, but deeds; not arguments, but the grace of God and his boundless compassion, for which we must pray. Therefore we can only pray: 'Lead us not into temptation'; but we cannot refute the temptation with reasons. This prayer, and his teaching of how we should pray, is the only weapon which Jesus gives us. There is no other. There is no Confession and no theology, nothing at all that has to do with *Logos* and '-ology', which will help us to combat temptation. For we ourselves and our thoughts are all on its side. In the last resort they all pull the same way as he who began in the garden of Eden to pull and to talk. The only one who is against it is God himself and his word. And thus we can only beg him: 'May the right man fight for us.' For we have no adequate weapon of our own, nor are we capable of wielding such a weapon; here we ourselves are the battleground.

16. *Hunger and Doubt*

All this we learn from Jesus' first temptation: this temptation does not arise out of thoughts; the tempting thoughts arise out of a reality—the concrete reality of hunger. And is not hunger something which touches the greatest reality of our life—our communion or our break with God? When our stomach is

growling are we ready for prayer? And if we are completely
starving? Does not communion with God die then? Do not
feelings of piety and religion die when we do? Do not our gods
also starve? Must they not share in starvation and death when
the people who worshipped them are perishing, or when the
cultures, in whose framework they lived, are upset (cp. Spengler's
account of Christianity in his *Decline of the West*)? So those who
regard religion as a mythology proclaim, so they explain their
own doctrine of the primacy of the biological life-substance
over religion.

All these are tempting thoughts which arise from the reality
'hunger'. And when, in addition, there are thoughts inspired
by the Evil One, by means of which he probes the sore and weak
spots of our life, it is only to be expected that temptation strikes
to the very roots of life through things which concern its sus-
tenance and satisfaction, even its destruction and starvation,
with the result that doubting and tempting thoughts rise like
bubbles of gas in a marsh.

Jesus knows this when he teaches us to say the Lord's Prayer,
for in it he links the prayer for daily bread with the prayer for
the kingdom of God. This shows us how highly the realism of the
divine thought values our concrete bodily existence, and how
high the body stands in his view. Did not the eternal Word
itself become flesh and tie itself to this our earth? Here in the
body, in the reality of our life, where it is a matter of eating or
starving, is the most vulnerable spot for the thrust of the tempter.
Thence arise the most tempting thoughts. There, perhaps, is
the spot where the Marxist man suffered his first temptation—
if we wish tentatively and daringly to speak of this, for once.
'First comes eating, then come morals.'

Temptation always arises in a concrete situation in our life.
And yet it must be noted that even the brutally physical side of
life is not the ultimate ground of temptation. The ultimate
ground is the still deeper, still more real reality of our communion with God and our break with God. This reality, that
our communion with God is lost or jeopardised—that we are
wandering in exile (prodigal sons) and our lives are no longer
rooted in God—is the true ground of all temptation, the cause
of our being tempted, beaten and broken.

Beside this reality, those other external realities—for instance, brutal threats to our physical existence, sickness, hunger, the thousand strains to which we are subjected—are only opportunities for that abysmal power to break in; they are only the *means* utilised by the tempter of Job and of Jesus Christ and of all the prophets and the children of men. And the earthly ministers of this great adversary are also very willing to use this means at all times and places, 'tightening the belt', using the instruments of terror and the threat to existence, in order to tempt the servants of God. But those means could not affect us if we were not temptable, if we did not live in an age which is on its way from the Fall to the Judgment.

That is the great lesson taught us by the hunger of our Lord; that the tempter takes hold of him through his concrete life and not through sophisticated theoretical questions. At this point we can only recognise reverently and with consoling certainty how deeply God plunged him into the flesh; for it is in this his flesh, in his and our body, that he experiences temptation; it is here, and not in his head which touches the stars that the crisis begins in his communion with God.

At no point does Jesus' temptation come so near to us as here. A temptation which consisted merely of feelings and ideas would remain foreign to us. For different people have different feelings and ideas. But everyone knows or can guess what hunger and bodily necessity are, what pain and the fear of death are. As our brother, Jesus Christ underwent temptation to set us an example; he learnt to know pain and temptation from his body, from the 'problem of existence'.

He has lived before us and suffered before us.

Temptation due to the great realities, blows of fate, injustices, earthquakes, wars, revolutions—he endured all this in that hour.

This temptation consisted in the failure of God to answer, in the great silence surrounding God, who kept him waiting 'senselessly' in the hour of hunger, and did not raise bread for him out of the stones.

'God keeps silence!'—that is the great temptation in those realities.

Could God really keep silent on the East-West question? Could he keep silent about the earthquake in Lisbon? Could he keep silent about the violent end of a rich young life? Can it be possible that God would keep silent—if he really were God?

17. *The Devil on the Basis of the Fact of God*

—If there were a God: that is the second thing that determines the tempter's question.

'If there is a God, he must give you bread now. . . . If you are the Son of God, then you must now be able to tell these stones to become bread.'

What is of decisive importance in this new thought is that the devil takes his stand on the basis of facts. He takes his stand, with cool effrontery, on the basis of God's existence. The serpent in paradise did that when it posed the tempter's question: 'Hath God said —— ?' The question means this: 'Dear Eve, we will not argue about God. He is a fact with which we must reckon (the words drip like balm into Eve's pious soul!). I won't argue with you either as to whether he really spoke, whether there is such a thing as "God's word" (what more can one want, enquires Eve gleefully; why not joyfully say yes and join the crowd?) Ah, no! dear Eve, I take my stand on the basis of these positive facts. But I must talk to you about another point— quite objectively and with no wish to entrap you. I must ask you precisely what he said—whether, for instance, he said, "ye shall not eat of every tree in the garden" ' (Gen. 3.1).

'Well now,' continues the serpent, 'even if he did say this, I am prepared to take up my stand with you on the basis of the facts, namely, the fact of this "word". For a serious person, conscious of his responsibilities, must still ask himself what he meant by that word, whether it is to be understood literally, or only in a general sense, and whether in your case it must not be applied quite differently' (Gen. 3.5).

After this fashion the serpent converses with the woman, and gazes movingly up to heaven as he speaks, then firmly closes his mouth—a picture of solicitude and understanding.

The serpent is assuredly not the Bolshevik type of atheist who blurts out his infernal notions in Paradise—the serpent is a firm believer in God. Indeed he is fully informed on the subject of God—and he trembles (Jas. 2.19). But being cunning and clever, he succeeds in trembling with his tail only, while his face remains calm, compelling and fascinating. At all events he takes his stand on the basic fact of 'God'. For that very reason is he so sinister, so dangerous, so abysmal, so hellish, because he goes to work from that standpoint—does he not on that account wear the mask of an angel of light (2 Cor. 11.14)?

He goes even further! He actually takes his stand—and why not?—on the fact that Jesus is the Son of God. In the conditional clauses ('if thou . . . ') the seducer makes full allowance for this. He is quite prepared for Jesus to set about proving that he is the Son of God—he has only cast doubt on that for tactical reasons—and to perform a few representative miracles. The tempter is not so ill-mannered as to make fun of the Lord or laugh at him because he fails to perform the miracle.

The tempter has no intention of exposing Jesus and destroying his reputation in this way. His intentions throughout are quite definite and deliberate. His aim lies in another direction. His aim is precisely to incite Jesus to miracle-mongering in proof of the fact that he is God's Son. But why? What possible advantage could he, the devil, gain from this? No less indeed than this: it would then be he, the devil, who would prescribe Christ's action. It would then be he who held the real power. It would then be in his name and to his glory that the miracles would be worked; in his name and to his glory—how horrible even to think of it!—that Jesus would be the Son of God.

That is the terrifying consequence of the devil's taking his stand on the fact of God. That is why his disguise is so dangerous. For this reason is he so dangerous a seducer, a 'teacher of error' in the Church, because there his principle of taking his stand on the fact of God, on the basis of positive Christian belief, is seen at its most effective. We may well say that the most diabolical thing about the devil is that he takes this stand. That is why he is accounted a liar from the beginning. That is why he is called the 'ape' of God. That is why we can mistake him for God.

18. *Calculator and Intriguer*

We must now conscientiously enquire as to the manner in which the tempter takes his stand on the fact of God, and how, for instance, it differs from the stand taken by Jesus.

The distinction seems to be this: the devil takes his stand *upon* but not in submission to the fact of God. He does not subordinate himself to God, like a servant or a son, but remains (as far as he is able) beyond God's jurisdiction, looking at him from outside. He does not submit to God—he tries conclusions with him. He regards God as a clever chess-player does his pieces, or, better still perhaps, the board on which he plays. God is an important factor, the supreme factor in the game: only to that extent does the devil acknowledge the bitter fact of God's existence. This simply means that he takes account of God as a fact to be reckoned with in the course of the game and which he, as a diabolical player, must view from the outside. 'From the outside'—because he does not see it as one who looks from God's house, illumined by God's light (Ps. 36.9); he does not see it with the eyes of a son or a servant (John 10.27; 18.37) —he sees it from hell, for what is hell other than this being 'outside God', this simple fact of being shut out?

'If God is God and you are his Son, then he and you must draw the following conclusions. Yes, my dear chap, I mean conclusions, for I like to express myself logically and precisely, in terms which are at once popular and scientific. Now here, for example, in the desert, the conclusion might be drawn that you should make bread . . . '

Thus does the devil chop logic and play chess with God. Thus, from outside, he sets his hand on the pieces, both human and divine. It is worth while to illustrate the seducer's method by an example from logic: in his evil hands God becomes a mere premise in a syllogism—for the devil does reckon with the fact of God—a premise from which we can draw the conclusions which suit us. And what could have been more pleasing to the hungry man Jesus than that the argument should run thus? From the fact of God, it follows that I should have bread. From the fact of God, it follows that the righteous man should prosper and that he should not go hungry. From the fact of God it follows that piety is bliss and not, humanly speaking, a senseless adventure with the Unknown. Must not everyone who says A go on to B? And must not everyone who says 'God' go on to say the rest—'bread, righteousness, peace'?

And thus, in the fashion of an arithmetical sum, clothed in the slick propositions of philosophical logic or of natural commonsense, the seducer goes on and on:

'If there were a god, then surely his Christians should look happier.

'If there were a god of love, then there could be no wars, no natural calamities, no cancer, no lunatic asylums.

'If there were a god of righteousness, then a lightning-flash must descend and transfix murderers, shedders of blood, offenders against conscience in every age and in every region of the earth—then truly world history would be the story of universal justice.'

Must not Jesus have seen the tempter's first question against the background of all these other questions and speculations? Must he not have discerned at the tempter's heels the gloomy swarm of doubts and temptations which now truly fills the air (Eph. 2.2) and strikes, as with the beaks of countless hawks, at the unprotected consciousness of mankind?

Yes indeed, Christ saw all this in that hour which, next to the crucifixion, was the darkest in his life. And we can say that in that hour he began his *via crucis* and took upon his shoulders in one first mighty effort the sin and the doubts of the world.

That hour in the desert leads straight to the other hour, when the sun veiled its light and the veil of the temple was rent. For then the tempter came once again in the darkness of night to the cross and skilfully formulated a proposition based on the fact of God. It was a powerfully compelling one: 'If thou art the Son of God, come down . . . '—'Do you not see, crucified sufferer, that it follows from your vocation that you must come down and lead us, and set up the kingdom of God.'—'Don't you see, church of the cross, don't you see, persecuted little flock, that you do not belong among the evil-doers and enemies of the state among whom you are reckoned? Don't you see how the Almighty blesses your persecutors and desires to be praised in the glory of their victories and triumphs?—So here is your place, church. To God and you and your master belongs the place of honour in history. And this place of honour is there, where the honoured and idolised sit. You must seat yourself beside them. You may gladly proclaim your allegiance to them, for God has blessed them. And from this sanction of blessing it follows that you belong among them, as the church of this God.'

'God is a God of light. Thence it follows that you are destined to live on the sunny side of life, beside kings and great ones, beside the wise and the strong, where the *vox populi* rings loud and praises the *vox Dei* which speaks out of it. That's where

you belong, there. For from God there follows—glory, not a
cross. From God follows—unity with the world, not revolt and
judgment. Therefore, you church of the Son of God, come
down, come down!'

And now Jesus confronts this chain of argument which seems
so devastatingly correct.

But he knows that these inferences (so astonishingly correct!)
from the premise 'God' appeal not only to the man in him, but
above all to the devil. For what could be better for the devil
than to let the Son of God be indeed the Son of God, just as a
victorious revolutionary may keep a king as his puppet, while
prescribing his actions? What could suit him better than to have
the Son of God in his power and make him dance to his piping?

He has a bright vision of bliss. He thinks he is looking into
the future, into an age full of triumphs which will all follow on
the one victory which he is just on the point of gaining. His lips
move gently, for he is impelled to put into words the infatuating
vision of this hour.

'The Son of God and his church shall dance to my piping!
They shall be found on the sunny side of life, on the side of
success, on the side of the big bosses, bestowing upon them the
blessing of religion. Yes; I will dictate the actions of the Son
of God and his church; I will decide what the Almighty must
bless, and to what the church must say Amen; I will decide
how the church is to be conceived and what follows from this
conception. I will decide how the results of all this shall affect
the life and doctrine of the church, its public function, and its
whole relation to that kingdom whose lord I am, namely the
world.'

19. *The Devil's Consistency*

Jesus sees all this. He sees how jealously anxious the devil is
to get into his hands the control of action, based on the fact of
God. He sees through the workings of his strategy, with its calculations which come out with such amazing success: 'From
God it follows . . .'. But he knows too that here the devil is
bluffing. He knows that he who deduces these devilish conse-
quences from the premise of 'God' has already deliberately falsi-
fied it.

What the devil means by God and the Son of God is not

God at all, but a puppet whom the devil, to suit his own purposes, can cause to jump and dance and make bread and come down from his cross. This God is not Lord of the devil, but his slave. The devil uses him to turn to his own account the great things of life and to sanction them with his stolen name.[1] In making his God of the apple dance like a marionette on silken threads and dictating to him what he shall do, this clever strategist is using him to get human beings into his power.

He uses him as opium for the people, to glorify in the name of religion the rulers of this world. He uses him as a means of cementing and uniting men in the name of religion. He uses him as the theme of mythically religious cults, in which the ages worship the idol of their equality with God, and celebrate the high mass of their immortality. The devil does all this under cover of biblical and Christian phrases, and he can turn Christianity into a myth and an opiate in the same way. He uses it over and over again. And the eyes of those whom, as lord of his world he deludes, no longer see the blasphemy implied in this use of the divine majesty as means to an end, and no longer perceive the horrible reversal of the truth: from him and through him and for him are all things. To him be glory for ever. Amen. (Rom. 11.36).

The tempter indeed plays a shrewd game. He knows that if people do not desire to exist for God, but think that God should exist for them (just as the economy exists—rightly—for the people and not *vice versa*), then the people are on his, the Evil One's, side; then they live sunk in their orgiastic cult and their pious recitation of sacred words—to the greater glory of blasphemy.

That is the tempter's final proposition in the series that begins

---

[1] There seems, according to Goethe, not only to be
'a law
Binding on ghosts and devils, to withdraw
The way they first stole in' (*Faust* I.3)
but also a law that the Evil One works through his agents and does not appear in person (as in the case of the Apple-God); and this reminds us of the tyrant characterised by Iphigenia in Goethe's play:
'a king who meditates
A deed inhuman, may find slaves enow,
Willing for hire to bear one half the curse
And leave the monarch's presence undefiled.
Enwrapt in gloomy clouds he forges death,
Whose flaming arrow on his victim's head
His hirelings hurl; while he above the storm
Remains untroubled, an impassive god.'
(*Iphigenie auf Tauris*, V.3)

with 'if'. And this time the premise and its inference are sound. But he does not pronounce this proposition aloud. He says it only to himself, in his inner triumph, or buries it in the blackest depths of his own soul. For this proposition depending on 'if' is the cunning point of his attacks, and a clever strategist does not betray his strategy; that is his secret. And we should not know it to this day, if Christ had not stood here in the desert and then hung on the cross, and if he had not in struggle and suffering emptied out the lowest depths of the tempter's black soul, and revealed it to all the world.

We now understand the answer to the tempter's first question: the tempter only seems to take his stand on the fact of God. In reality he is only using pious words, and speaking of God and God's Son and religion, 'from outside', from a place where God is not acknowledged consistently and categorically, even though he is known (and trembled at!) a thousand times—from a place where there is not a breath of that Spirit in whose name alone we can call Jesus Lord and Son of God (1 Cor. 12.3)—namely from Hell.

And in the fire of this hell all ideas are recast: God becomes —secretly—the antithesis of God. Christ becomes servant of the demonic glory. The cross loses its power.

This is not merely symbolic. In fact, the true hell in this story is that the temptation begins with the words '*If* thou art the Son of God', and that it ends with '*If* thou wilt fall down and worship me'.

Both are the peace-terms of the same dark power. But see, it is rendered powerless.

20. *The Obedience of Jesus*

This is the argument that Jesus opposes to the inferences made by the devil: 'It is written that man shall not live by bread alone, but by every word which proceedeth out of the mouth of God.' True, hunger cries out in him. And as he himself represents man, his hunger stands for all the strains and stresses by which man is assailed. Therefore not his own hunger alone cries out within him, but also all the torments of man—disease and pain and suffering, the misery of prisons and asylums, the bloodshed of war, the senselessness of so many things and the tears of an infinite number of nights.

The hunger of the Son of God is an uncanny hunger; for it embodies the torment of all the temptation which springs from the suffering of mankind. He bears indeed the suffering of the world. The hour of the cross has begun. This is its first moment.

Hunger indeed cries out in him. But he knows that the creation of bread will neither still it nor support us. It is not the fruits of the field, nor the splendid crops through which we walk, gratefully and reverently, in the summer that feed us, but God alone, through them. They are the agents of his kindly hand.

This we express in our harvest thanksgiving, for we do not thank the farmer, or our fruitful Mother Nature, but include them along with the whole cosmos in our prayers of thanks for the ineffable goodness of the Lord who has opened his hand and filled all things living with plenteousness (Ps. 145.16; 104.28). 'We plough the fields and scatter . . .'[1]

21. *The Masks of God*

It would be a grave sin (which is also allowed for in the devil's calculations) if we were to mistake our hands and the food which they hold for God himself; that would amount to the defilement of our daily bread. But this faith in the bread itself, instead of in the Father who gives it to his children (Matt. 6.31f), lies in wait for us, like faith in creation instead of in the creator, faith in the farmer instead of in the Lord of the farmer. 'Verily, verily I say unto you, ye seek me, not because ye saw the signs, but because ye did eat of the loaves, and were filled,' cries Jesus (John 6.26) in bitterness after the miraculous feeding of the five thousand. In the evil hands of men the miracle loses its transparency; they no longer see the master behind it, who uses it as a sign which should lead them to praise God; they have only the pleasant feeling of perfect, lip-smacking satiety, and thus the belly becomes their god and with

---

[1] [The well-known translation by J. M. Campbell of this hymn differs so considerably from the original, that the point made by Thielicke here is lost: a prose translation of Matthias Claudius's poem is therefore given:

We plough, and we scatter the seed on the land. But growth and thriving lie in Heaven's hand. It opens mildly and secretly, and with gentle breezes drips down growth and thriving, when we have gone home.

It sends dew and rain and sunshine and moonlight; it wraps up right tenderly and skilfully the blessing of God, and brings it then swiftly into our fields and our bread: it passes through our hands, but comes from God.—Tr.]

it the bread—which means that they praise the gift of God
instead of the Giver.

The tempter deals with the gift of God exactly as he does
with God himself. Here, too, he takes his stand on facts. Of
course he would be delighted to declare, as soon as Jesus had
made bread out of the stones: 'This is thy work and thus also
God's gift (for thou art the Son of God). Thus thou mayst still
thy hunger with it.'

But, all the same, there would have been one difference in
this gift of God produced by the devil, and this difference would
have made it into a gift of the devil: it would have been snatched
from God; it would have been turned into a sign of disobedience
and lack of trust. For Jesus would in his hunger have trusted
more in bread than in God. He would no longer have dared to
believe that man lives by every word that proceeds out of the
mouth of God, and that this word can preserve and feed in the
manifold ways open to the divine 'Let there be . . . ', of which
bread is only one (Mark 8.1-9; Exod. 16). He would no longer
have sought first the kingdom of God and righteousness, and
let bread and fish, butter, meat and shelter 'be added unto'
him (Matt. 6.33). No, with greed and with little faith he would
have grasped at these 'additional' gifts, and with his free hand
—he was after all Son of God—he would have striven to uphold
the kingdom as 'thrown into the bargain'; and so this kingdom
would really have been divided against itself (Mark 3.24-6). For
the tempter would have broken the chains of hell and stepped
into the arena with a heavy foot; he would have become the
secret usurper of the kingdom.

The tempter would in this way have succeeded, by taking his
stand on the fact of God, in falsifying not only God but his
gifts as well. There is nothing between heaven and earth—no
human work, no noble will, no gift of creation, nay, not even
the house of God (1 Pet. 4.17) which he would not have seized
upon with diabolical malice, and which would not have yielded
helplessly to his mastery—so far at least as its own strength
was concerned.

But the devil is beaten in this cunning attempt; Jesus does
that quite simply by suppressing the thought of hunger and
seeking protection in the stronghold of God and in his promise,
by taking his stand upon that word which proceeds out of God's

mouth, as upon a defiant fortress. For indeed, in this word
there blows the breath which creates men and things and renews
the face of the earth (Ps. 104.30). In this word thoughts are
formulated which are higher than our thoughts of bread, fish
and meat, and paths are trodden which are higher than our ways
of care and work (Isa. 55.8ff). Certainly we do not know these
ways and these thoughts by which he leads us. We do not know
the place and time and manner in which God nourishes us.
No, we often see only moving mountains and falling hills (Isa.
54.10), and a countenance hidden in wrath (Isa. 54.8). Often
we see and feel only the hunger. But we know the aim that
God pursues and the promise that is given to our faith: whatever ways the Father goes and whatever means he uses, whatever appears to hang in front of God's love like a gloomy cloud
(Rom. 8.35, 38f), it is nevertheless love, which does not let fall
the covenant of his peace (Isa. 54.10), and which brings it about
that the story of his salvation, in spite of all the confusions of
men, ends at his throne (1 Cor. 15.28). It is he who makes our
cheeks fresh and red, who gives pasture to cows and bread to
children, and gives to his own not a serpent but a fish, and not
a stone, but bread (Matt. 7.9). God does not want us to believe
in the _means_ whereby he supplies our daily needs—lest we think
we can live by bread alone; he wants us to believe in him like
beloved children and say to him: 'Thou hast no lack of means.'
He means exactly what Jesus says to the devil: that we must
submit ourselves wholly to God's promise and to his fatherly
kindness and approval. And that means that we do not live by
bread but by the word of God which promises us bread and
life, and makes the fields shimmer with gold in summer-time.

22. _The Spirit of Worry_

Thus we can be hungry and see no way of solving our prob-
lems, whether they relate to politics or church or private life,
we may be weighed down by our world with its gloomy prospects, without becoming little of faith or worrying about ways
and means.[1] We can walk on the waves without losing faith

[1] Only fools can think that we are here recommending a quietistic indifference,
or an attitude of facile optimism in political matters. On the contrary, this
absence of worry, or—better—this calm certainty about the highest things of life
sets us free to look about us and decide on a clear-cut plan of action without being
confused, worried and distracted by the will-o'-the-wisps of less important things.

and looking round—even before we feel ourselves sinking—for the ways of escape and the life-buoys on which we had set our hope (Matt. 8.25; 14.22ff).

This spirit of worry which pervades our life is the spirit of little or wrong faith. For worry always concentrates on what seems to be the sole means of getting rid of our worry; we are worried about means of sustaining life, financial or political means, as representing the only means of safety—i.e. the way out sought by the lack of a way out. We are living by bread alone; worry is nothing else but the worship of these means— the worship of bread, or of the earthly lord of bread, who can put us on short rations.

Thus it becomes completely clear why worry is a result of wrong faith or lack of faith. In the practical affairs of our life it is precisely what idolatry is in the religious sphere—the worship of the creature instead of the Creator, of the help instead of the helper, of the means instead of the Lord, of the medicine instead of the physician, of the bread instead of the Father who cares for us. On all counts it is lack of faith and the worship of idols which are the governing powers of our lives. When we drive God out of the door, ghosts come in at the window—the ghosts of worry and of other gods.

Is it not right to have gods and worship them? But the Evil One kneels beside us. Is it not right to make bread (of course, in the name of God) and to worship it? And yet it is the Evil One who made the bread into God and with a pious gesture set it in his place. God is slain by the bread which he was going to break for his children. That is the sign of Cain on the forehead of worry.

23. *The Battle-fronts in our Breast*

The great confession which Jesus proclaims here is: 'It is God's promise alone which keeps me. By it I live in faith, and not by gazing at bread. Nay, I see no bread and am starving; I see no water and am dying of thirst; I see no men who believe in me, and yet I am to bring them the kingdom.

'I see, like Abraham, no country and no friendship and no children (Gen. 12.1ff), and yet I believe in thy promise that thou wilt give me children like the sand of the sea and the stars in the heaven. Thy word alone shall lead my fears and hopes;

thy promise alone, thy grace alone, dear Father; thou alone art always my hope' (Gen. 15.2). Jesus does not believe in bread but in the promise; he believes in 'every word that proceedeth out of the mouth of God'. And if this word now gives him bread in his great hunger, he will thank God, break it and eat with gladness. The connexion between all this and the evangelical 'by faith alone', 'by grace alone' must be obvious to everyone. And if the same word refuses him the loaf, he will go on hungering and believing in God's promise that he is destined to a great work and will not die of hunger. The very word of God is the Lord in this hour, and Jesus lives by it.

And so the remarkable and miraculous thing appears: Jesus does no more than allow this word to answer the challenge of the tempter; he allows himself to be nothing more than a faithful follower of his commander. It is not the courage of disciplining hunger, it is not the power or the joy of resistance, that he opposes to the tempter—and yet who would dare to deny that he incidentally possessed all this too at that hour? But all this is mere 'flesh and blood' and cannot resist the tempter. For temptation differs from all other conflicts and contestants by being enacted within man and by dividing the heart of man into two fronts: as, for instance, into the front which upholds 'loyalty to the promise, loyalty to the faithfulness of God', and the doubting front which asks, 'Can God really interpret his promise in such a way that you must now die of hunger, rather than that bread should be promised you now, so that you need only say to these stones: "Become bread!"?'

This conflict is the reverse of all others—we are not drawn up in one battle-front, awaiting the advance of the opposing front, as if we were Christ, for instance, awaiting the advance of Antichrist, or as if we were no longer of this world and the world itself were marching against us.

Yes, if it were like this, courage and the will to attack could help.

Unfortunately, this is not the case; our enemy does not attack us from without—the attack takes place within our own breast; Antichrist and the world are within our breast, and the demarcation-line between them and us passes right through our own heart; we are the world and the kingdom of God; we are righteous men and sinners at one and the same time. That is

the real conflict: we are always in the midst of temptation, and
the tempter is already within our hearts. He comes not as a
foe, but as a friend. And so he has stolen keys and an entry-
permit, and is inside. He takes his stand, now as always, on the
fact of God. He obligingly said what we had always thought:
'Did God really say this? Did he not mean it thus? Would it
not suit him if you now did this and that, instead of taking his
word all too literally?'

Further, the tempter is so deep within our own hearts that
his voice is indistinguishable from the voice of these hearts
themselves, and from the whispering and murmuring of our
blood. He is as completely inside as Christ will be inside later,
and as we shall be in Christ. For we are always in the service
of a Lord (Matt. 6.24).

24. *The Cosmic Spectacle*

In such times as these, which one of us has not felt again and
again that our faith and our loyalty slip through our fingers like
sand, which not even the strongest fist can hold fast? But, were
it otherwise, could we give God the same loyalty that we give
to a flag, with which we can commit ourselves to stand or fall?
If we could, then to be a Christian would merely be easy, or
difficult, as the case might be. But that is just what we cannot
do. Our own strength will by no means suffice to keep us loyal.
For all these ideological and political myths and cults are our
own myths and cults; indeed, they are our own hearts—or, as the
theologian puts it, the natural man, the Old Adam, speaking.
And these secret whisperings of our own heart advance against
us from the opposing ranks of anti-Christian doctrines and
human myths, but in a more organised and overwhelmingly
powerful form, metamorphosed into a flag and an open confession of allegiance.

Therefore we cannot resist with flesh and blood; for our front
is broken up, and this world lies in the twilight between God
and Satan.

The abyss of temptation yawns not before but within us;
therefore we cannot be true to God, but God must be true to us.
We cannot hold his hand, but he must hold our hand. We
cannot fight for him but he must fight for us. We can only say:
'May the right man fight on our side.' Therefore we cannot

love God, but he must first love us (1 John 4.19). And only after all this has befallen us, has happened to us out of God's unfathomable goodness, only after he has made known his faithfulness to us and has made the ages revolve until they brought Christmas to this poor earth, only now can we say: 'Let us love him . . . ' (1 John 4.19). 'Now be thou, too, faithful unto death' (Rev. 2.10). 'Now praise thou, too, God in thy spirit and in thy body' (1 Cor. 6.20). 'Now take thou, too, the shield of faith, with which thou canst quench all the fiery darts of the enemy' (Eph. 6.16), for lo, all this has happened to thee. . . .

Because our flesh and blood are become powerless in themselves, Jesus teaches us not to resist the tempter in our own name, but to call the divine Helper to our aid. He teaches us to say, 'Lead us not into temptation but deliver us from evil', so that the helper may keep us and fight for us, and then—and not until then!—we may march behind as faithful soldiers. 'It is a poor soldier who hangs back when he sees his commander going forward.'

At this point we realise the full implication of Jesus' words to the tempter.

In the midst of temptation, in the midst of this conflict of the powers in whose line of fire he stands, between the abyss of death by hunger and the abyss of disobedience in the guise of obedience—among all these perils, and truly 'de profundis'—he calls upon God's word and upon God's promise, that it may swallow up the tempter, and steps trustingly into the shadow and shelter of this word. He believes God even when he sees no bread.

25. *Our Pleading and God's Majestic Will*

Jesus has set us an example by putting his trust in his heavenly Father amid pain and suffering. In addition he teaches us to base our life and our prayers on that same trust.

We may ask for daily bread. We may ask for help and ways of escape from our distress. Best of all, we may talk to our Father in heaven. We may tell him of the ways in which we think he can help us. We may ask for daily bread for our hunger, work for our working days, calm in our anxiety, health in our illness, a friend in our loneliness. We may ask him for all these things, and talk to him about them as children talk to their father. And yet he taught us always to begin our plea with the words: 'Thy will be done'; and to accept one condition: 'If it be thy will' (Luke 22.42)—and then we may boldly pray that the stones may turn into bread.

But is this prayer, 'Thy will be done', not after all a secret surrender of what one has just prayed for or is about to pray for? That is not the case. It does not mean: 'I am not happy about my petition, dear heavenly Father. . . . It was intended only provisionally, and I would rather take it back. . . . Yes, Father, I renounce my bread. Thy will shall not be bound by my little wishes. Thy will shall sweep onwards great and sublime over my little, little affairs.'

This is just what the words 'Thy will be done' do not mean. They mean: 'Thou understandest my prayer better than I understand it myself (Rom. 8.26). Thou knowest whether I most need hunger or bread. Whatever may come, I will still say "Yes, dear Lord" (Matt. 15.27). For I know that in everything no matter what it may be, thy will gives me fulfilment—beyond my asking and my comprehension' (Eph. 3.20).

In these four little words, 'Thy will be done', therefore, I say exactly what the Saviour says in the desert, when he says: I live by the word of God; I live by his promise, no matter how that promise may be fulfilled—whether the stones become bread, or whether they remain stones, and whether or not help unexpectedly arrives in time of need.

These four little words mean simply this: 'I live by thy will, dear Lord. And I know that this will desires nothing else but to fulfil thy promise. Yes, Lord, thy will is thy promise. Therefore I do not live by bread alone. I have prayed for what is best for me, that thou mayest preserve my life and give me my daily bread. And I know, dear Lord, that thy will, which shall be done—from my heart I pray that it shall be done—decides what is best for me and sends hunger or bread according to which can serve me for my good (Rom. 8.28). Therefore I know that my petition finds its fulfilment.'

The Lord's Prayer, which Jesus prays as an example to us, is also acted out by him before us in the desert. He lives by every word which comes from God. He lives by the will of God as that will is being carried out. He lives by God's promise. What he says to the devil is simply this: Look, I call into the arena him by whom I live. It is with him that you have to deal, and not with me. He is my sun and shield (Ps. 84.11). Look, I live by him entirely and not by your bread. For that reason —and for that reason alone—I am the Son of God. But you will never be able to understand that. How could you?"

THE SECOND TEMPTATION:

THE ALLURING MIRACLE OF DISPLAY

Then the devil taketh him into the holy city, and placeth him upon a pinnacle of the temple, and saith unto him, If thou art the Son of God, throw thyself down: for it is written, He shall command his angels concerning thee, and they will carry thee in their hands, lest at any time thou dash thy foot against a stone. Jesus said to him, Again it is written, Thou shalt not tempt the Lord thy God.

26. *The Honour of God and the Integrity of his Word*

WHAT the devil says is to all appearances very pious. He takes a further step based on the fact of God. For what is at stake now is not the honour of God's Son, but the honour of God himself: 'He shall command his angels concerning thee' (Matt. 4.6). God's power will be respected, which means (according to the logic of the tempter) that it will be allowed to 'work', and must be given 'expression'. But here it is not only of paramount importance that God himself is at stake—the God to whose honour the tempter seems to attach so much importance. He goes further, and reinforces his question with God's own words: 'It is written' (Ps. 91.11-12). Could more be done?

Why should Jesus not take him up? That would not, as in the case of the first question, contradict the promise! On the contrary it would enable a tremendously impressive demonstration of God's promise to be given. Why should he not leap from one of the pinnacles of the temple? Why should he not say in the name of God to one of the mountains (Matt. 17.20; 1 Cor. 13.2): 'Be thou removed and cast thyself into the sea'? Why should he not descend from the cross—*ad majorem Dei gloriam*?

And yet all this is nothing but the devil's question. How does that come about?

At this stage we will not again refer to the fact that with all his pious gestures and his holy words the devil only wants to gain the power of prescribing action; he wants to have God's power at *his* disposal, by appealing to God's 'ambition'. This tactic has already been abandoned—or has at least undergone modification—in his second question, even though, secretly and insidiously, its undertones remain.

In considering this second question, which is a kind of cunning and pious-seeming gamble with the power of God, we must remember a further point—that there *is* no such god as this God of Power. He is an imaginary idol of men. For this God of Power is a god of convenience; he has the power, and we use him (or do without him) just as here the devil deals in his own way with this God, or would like to do so.

27. *The Worshippers of the 'God of Power'*

We see at once why this is so. When we contemplate the worshippers of the God of Power, they are the fools who say in their heart: 'There is as good as no god; there is only a God of Power' (Ps. 14.1; 53.1). Who does not know these worshippers? Who has not talked to them? At what bar, at what party, at what mass-meeting can one not hear them?

They say that their god is exalted far above the human traits of a god who speaks and who is supposed to have left written evidence. They say that their God of Power looks down with scorn and irony upon the intimate relation in which the little people and the failures of this world think that they stand to their personal God, who has converse with men—as servants, as children, as friends, as sons (Gen. 18.3–Rev. 22.3; Isa. 45.11– Heb. 12.5; Exod. 33.11–Jas. 2.3; Deut. 1.31–Rev. 21.7).

But are this God of Power and his friends not very much to be suspected? The exalted nature of this God of Power assumes all too easily such gigantic proportions that he is also too exalted to concern himself with our private life. He cares nothing for sparrows, hairs, lilies, or the thoughts of our hearts, our secret or open rebellion; he cares nothing for will or deed, or any of the multitude of things which must remain hidden from the light of day. Certainly he is not asleep, nor does he go for walks, nor write poetry (1 Kings 18.27), but he is—exalted.

What else can explain the fact that these worshippers of the God of Power draw so amazingly few—in fact, none at all— inferences from this their God? How is it that one notices so little of him in their lives? How does it come about that with all his power he is so small a force, so slight a factor in the grey of their everyday life? How comes it that he is only mentioned at their festivals and in moods of emotion—real or fictitious—to provide the celestial setting and the golden background, the religious magic for their mood? (Up there above the canopy of stars must dwell a beloved Father.) How comes it that he only exists to countersign (as Providence) what men have already signed and sealed, and now would like to see sanctioned? How comes it that his followers are so little aware of his will and law and judgment in the decisive hours of life? How is it that his approval is only sought after the event, and then loudly proclaimed? His approval is sought for what is already a *fait accompli*, and therefore cannot be undone by him—his approval, in short, is sought for something which man, in spite of all his pious gestures, has manoeuvred according to his own sole judgment, and with which he will brook no interference (least of all from an authority beyond his control!).

How comes it that 'in the religious sphere' the more exalted God is, the less supervision he exercises over his worshippers, and that the litany inherent in his cult is a continual 'Let me alone'?

How comes it that the worshippers of the God of Power can always think that their God has to do with the Beyond, while their task is to shape this world? They know that one bird (of this world) in the hand is better than two birds (of the Beyond) in the bush.

Oh, yes! The worshippers of the God of Power understand something of the realities of this world: they reckon with God, they switch him on and off and liquidate him; they allow him to react with religious complexes which otherwise would become dangerous explosive material. (Is it not the repeated experience of history that, apart from the belly-question, nothing whips history forwards like the religious question?) These worshippers mix their God of Power with opium.

It is indeed a suspicious fact that even the devil in the wilderness knows the God of exaltedness, the God of Power, appeals joyfully to him and—unless appearances are deceptive—feels completely undisturbed by him. The devil seems to live quite comfortably under his protection. Why is this? Why should not such an exalted God permit himself the luxury of a devil?

Exaltedness means, among other things, embracing all possibilities. Why not also the possibility of the devil, of evil? Good
and evil, 'Deceit and truth are only the two-coloured blossoms on
the tree of humanity' (Albrecht Schaeffer: *Demetrius. A Tragedy*,
Act IV, Sc. 17 (p. 139)). Does this not apply much more to the
tree of God? Is not Mephistopheles a servant appointed by
his lord?

So it is that we are able to face this Exalted One, this God of
Power, with equanimity. He is a comfortable God. Each of us
longs for him in our tired hours—and in hours of savagery and
uncontrolled violence, in the hour when the blood pulses through
our veins and our nerves are feverishly wrought-up, and no God
can stand in our way. Through these hours vibrate the birth-
pangs of the God of Power; for this God is born of men. And
the devil knows, too, why he remains undisturbed by him, and
why he suggests to all his victims that he is their tempter. He
knows well enough, and possibly invented, the basic law of all
religion—that law which we find confirmed a thousand times
around and within us, and which could be formulated: The
more exalted the god of men is, the less compulsion does he lay
on men. He enforces his wishes less as the degree of his exaltedness increases. There is no need to be afraid of him, for he does
not meddle in earthly affairs. He is no more than a figure of
speech, incapable of motivating a single act. He is a mere
swelling of bombast, an empty tinkling of bells.

But God the Lord is not this God of Power; he is not the
'exalted one' with which we adorn our speeches and who so
fortunately demands nothing from us. No! *our* God has a will,
a holy will; he is the incarnation of majesty.

Nor can we say that the relation between ourselves and God
is never more than an impersonal mechanical relation, a mere
power ratio, namely the ratio between his infinite strength and
might and our pygmy impotence. (If that were so, why did
Jesus not lay claim to divine omnipotence and perform the
miracle of leaping from the temple?)

No, what confronts us here is not this kind of neutral ratio of
power, involving no obligation on either side, but the relation
of the One who demands to that which is demanded, of the
Holy to the unholy, of the Judge to the judged, and of the
Father to the children.

28. *Will and Power of God*

We describe all this somewhat abstractly when we speak of a 'personal God'—that is, of a God with whom we ourselves are personally concerned. This description makes clear the difference between this God and the God whose power is neutral and non-binding—the merely 'All-Powerful' God. We can best make clear to ourselves the infinite distance of God the Lord from this neutral Power-God by realising that God the Lord is *Will*, a personal will that demands something of us. That is why we pray to him: 'Thy will be done', and do not just say, as the unimplicated spectators of the contest for power say: 'Providence takes its course.'

The devil has nothing to say about the will of God. For he hates this will and categorically refuses to do its bidding. He refuses to stand 'under' God. He only stands 'on' the fact of God. He stands 'outside'—as we see—as the cunning observer, the mischief-maker and intriguer. That is his reason for speaking of the God of Power, who imposes no obligation, and with whom he can do as he likes. And that is also his reason for not speaking about the will of God, that total will which impounds us, takes control of us, and with which we just cannot do as we like. The devil knows that this will of God is the real danger-zone for him. He knows that he—devil as he is—only becomes completely the devil under this will; and he knows this as surely as he knows that he himself must now openly take the role of the adversary. Only face to face with holiness does the devil become completely devil. Only face to face with the law—and that means face to face with the incarnate majesty of God—does sin become completely sin (Rom. 7.13). In face of the Son of God the demons arise with double impetus (Matt. 8.29). Beneath this will the game is at an end. Under this will things become diabolically serious; life becomes frighteningly full of duty. Therefore—thus thinks the devil—he must get this will into his hands. He must get its power into his service. Here in the desert he has his best chance of doing so. It would be foolish and over-cynical to talk to this Son of God about the 'holy will of God'. 'Preaching doesn't suit me,' thinks the devil, 'and moreover I might show my most dangerous cards in doing it.' For this reason he keeps silence about the will of God, and prefers to talk of the God of Power. And for this reason he challenges this power. 'He will command his angels concerning thee . . . '.

If this ruse succeeds, his *coup d'état* has come off. Then he can dictate, as we saw, the law of action, and triumphs over the will of God. It is a fantastic possibility which the devil has here, a prospect such as no human being ever had: for men the God of Power is only a phantom of the brain, a pious dream, a tendentious fiction, an opiate for the people, and so on. But the devil has a chance of turning this imagined, fictitious God into a reality—truly a diabolical prospect. If he succeeds in tempting the Son of God to leap from the temple, the will of God is under his control, and he can drag it down to earth and into hell. He orders, and God acts. He commands, and the Son of God leaps, and the Father sends helping angels. Here the same thing that we saw earlier is seen from an even gloomier angle, for now God is really the will-less God of Power. The devil is now the will, and he possesses the power. He is now the mighty prime minister, and God is his royal puppet.

That is the secret of this hour: The Son of God, who brings the kingdom and the turning-point of the ages, stands before the Accuser, and is tempted. And in this hour this kingdom is in danger. Can there be a greater threat than this hour brings? To which of these two will the kingdom belong when this hour is past?

But Jesus tears from the tempter the secret that he has so craftily suppressed. He knows that he stands wholly under the will of his Father in heaven, that he has come to fulfil this will and his Father's command. He remembers, too, that no command of his Father's bids him leap from the pinnacle. He knows that he must never trifle with the power of his Father, nor with his own power—and that means that he must never do anything irresponsibly, merely for pleasure and without being commanded to do so. The legends that as a child Jesus moulded birds of clay and then made them alive are just legends and appear to have no solid foundation. Every moment of his life is lived by God's commandments and by his promise—and by these alone. This power of God obeys his command only, and is the instrument of his promise.

But Jesus knows with all certainty that he would injure, deride and blaspheme this will of God, if he were to leap down from the temple in the name of a supposed God of Power. For if he were to jump—in defiance of all commands—he would be putting God to the test; he would be looking inquisitively to see if angels would come to carry him down; it would be a moment of ineffable tension; it would be the test of the strength of God.

And in it the deep-seated motive driving him to this test of strength would become plain—distrust, lack of faith: 'Hath God said . . . ?' 'And if he did say so, can he really do what he said? I have a right to know. Yes; does not God owe me this? Does not God(!) owe me(!) this? Is not God my debtor? Am I not God's creditor, since he once made me in his image? Am I not equal with God? Have I not a right to know good and evil and to be immortal? Have I not also a right to use the power of God? May I not, *must* I not leap down? Who can forbid me to find out whether God is worthy of my trust—whether *God* is worthy of *me*—me who trust in him (provisionally!) to carry me down on the wings of his angels?'

These thoughts the tempter caused to pass slowly in rainbow colours through the soul of Jesus, each one by itself and one after the other. Then the desert was suddenly paradise, and beside him stood Adam and Eve. Before them hung the apple of the tree of life, lovely to see, inciting, full of promise. And in the same moment the pinnacles of the temple rose in light before God's Son, a paradisal sight, alluring, inciting and full of promise.

But at the very point where Adam and Eve gave in to the temptation, Jesus rises above it. Man 'liveth by every word that proceedeth out of the mouth of God'. In this hour he lives by the word: 'Thou shalt not tempt the Lord thy God.'

29. *The Godly Demon*

The terrible thing about the tempter's second question is that it is such a pious one. It is more pious than the first, because it goes to work not only with a religious phrase and the right and wrong use of the fact of God, but because it quotes the Bible and 'takes God at his word'. That is the most dangerous mask possessed by the devil: the mask of God. It is more horrifying than the garment of light. Luther knew something about it. He was dreadfully afraid of it. He saw himself as it were

encircled by God. He had to flee from God (from this masked
demon) to God. This flight is one of the ultimate secrets of his
faith. We must have stood in the desert beside Jesus Christ to
be aware of it. Luther, too, meets temptation with sayings from
scripture; he makes the Word fight for itself. But that is no
simple affair. For now he learns that the prince of demons who
has risen against him is so armed to the teeth with Bible-sayings
that his own knowledge of scripture melts away before him.
He must let the true Word fight for itself. He himself must be
the battlefield.

Yes; the word of God, piety, worship, religion, miracles and
signs are the mightiest weapons of the wicked foe. According
to the Revelation of St. John, this human representative of
Satan's dominion, the mighty champion of Antichrist on earth
is no enemy of religion, but one perfumed with the incense of
his worship and surrounded by the ordinances of the new religion, which penetrate the whole of life, so that no one can buy
or sell without the mark of this Lord (Rev. 13.11-17). And the
tempter is mightiest just where he seems to stand in the place of
God and of Jesus Christ, and people say: 'Lo, *here* is the Christ!
Lo, *there* he is!' (Matt. 24.23ff).

We must go deeper still into this secret of the power which
fights against God.

To all appearances it now becomes obvious that God can be
played against God; that it is possible to kill one word with
another: 'It is written', says the tempter. On the other hand,
'It is written', answers the Son of God. And here we could
go on for a long time, for here a secret of the word itself becomes obvious: 'It is written'; 'Work out (and that means:
ye work out) your own salvation with fear and trembling'
(Phil. 2.12).

'Again it is written': 'It is God that worketh in you both to
will and to do his good pleasure' (Phil. 2.13).

This phrase in the Letter to the Philippians explains the
secret which we have indicated here: here more than anywhere
else we have the possibility, and indeed the most tempting possibility, of playing God against God. We have it as soon as we
become onlookers, and once more dally with the devil's point
of view. And has it not always been so; have not heretics and
false teachers and demons always crept into the church with the

aid of that word, rather than with the aid of resounding anti-Christian slogans?

One party stands on the one side and says: Everything depends on our working with fear and trembling. Up, let us do 'good works'; we shall give the half of our goods to the poor (Luke 19.8), we shall keep the commandments: Thou shalt not commit adultery; thou shalt not steal; thou shalt not bear false witness; thou shalt not defraud; honour father and mother (Mark 10.19); we shall keep all this from our youth up (Mark 10.20); with fear and trembling we shall do it, for our salvation. More: with fear and trembling we shall go to seek God. He will be the conflict of our days and the longing of our nights. We shall send our souls to track down the Eternal, and shall not rest till God yields to our attack, till he becomes our prey—so that we may gain salvation.

But do we not feel when we speak in this way that we are blaspheming against God, and that this blasphemy is doubly horrible because it is committed in his name? Is God really an object to be fought for and striven after; and can we really force him into dependence on our achievement, and thus again secretly and cunningly gain power over him?

30. *The Word of God in the Twilight*

It is the same old story: If we are not obedient servants of this word who stand humbly beneath it, but have recourse to diabolical means to make it the slave of our own desires (so that we think that *our* works, done with fear and trembling, or *our* Faustian urge, could sway God, this divine word turns in our hands to a rending, tearing demon, which thrusts these hands upwards till they become fists clenched against God. And we can still think—we who are 'justified' by good works, guilty of the theft of Prometheus, misled by the devil—that by greeting God with that raised fist we are doing him a 'divine service'.

The opposing party stands on the other side and says: 'No, it is God, who works in us both to will and to act. Away with your striving and God-seeking, away with your "works"! We perform the true service of God; we surrender ourselves to God's creative will; we lay our hands in our lap and wait for the great miracle—that God should come, that he should speak to us.

And when he comes, we shall feel his secret working in our souls. What can we do now, anyway?'

And so they too falsify this word of God and assail him with his own speech. They play God against God. And the lookers-on at the kingdom of God shrug their shoulders and say: 'You can prove anything with words from the Bible.' And in fact this popular slogan proclaims that abysmal truth, the truth that we *can* play God against God.

The devil again proceeds on his principle of working as spectator and logician: 'From the fact of God it follows.' And thus there follows, or is alleged to follow, from the fact of God, either what the Bible brands as righteousness based on the Law or on works and as a blasphemous attempt to dominate God by force or the attitude expressed by the quietistic doctrine which bids us lay our hands in our lap and with a delusive sense of 'resting in God', let everything take its course.

The great seducer always uses the same devices: he seems to take God at his word, and yet he twists the meaning of this word almost before it has left God's mouth. For we can only take God at his word by placing ourselves under and not above this word. Only thus do we learn the connexion between the imperative, the command of the holy God: 'Work, *you* work!' and the indicative, the statement: 'It is I who work in you, both in will and in deed. I am the alpha and the omega, and I am the ocean that beats from all sides on the shore of your age.'

Who would dare to say before this living God: 'Thou doest all things; therefore I am free of responsibility'; 'For it is thou who every time hast caused me to become guilty'? Or who would dare to say before the living God: 'Thou thyself hast told me to work. So just let me carry on alone. I can be saved without thee; I can get right without thee'? Surely no one who stands before God, and is humbled under the sharp, two-edged sword of his word.

Only here, confronted by the word of God and humble in the face of his inexpressible authority, do we learn how the truth of God always stands on two feet: on the promise: Ye are dead to the Law through my grace (Gal. 2.19), and at the same time on the command: Therefore be now of yourselves and be in fact slaves of righteousness (Rom. 6.4ff). Or: Ye are bought with a price, therefore lead your lives in a way befitting the

E

property of God, which means: Praise God in your body and in your spirit, which are God's (1 Cor. 6.20).

And in this obedience, in this humility, we come to understand that there is a connexion between the issues fought out in the desert. God gives his angels charge of his son; nevertheless the Son of God can be required not to invoke this aid, but to go his way quietly and do only what he is commanded to do.

Thus Jesus' answer must be incomprehensible to the devil, who does not stand under the word of God, but kneads it into diabolical shapes, as we might mould a lump of clay. He picks out the 'appropriate texts' and fits them together as a child does the bricks in his toy-box. What philosophical and heretical system of the Occident has not appealed to the Bible in this same sense?

31. *The Word as Authority*

But how could Jesus assume that this particular Bible text which he uses would have more authority than all the rest, and would not be suspected of being arbitrarily selected: 'With the Bible one can prove anything'? He might have said: 'With the Bible I can now prove—thank goodness—that I do not need to try out that dangerous leap from the temple-pinnacle, that venture of faith; I can prove that indeed I *must* not! What luck that this text occurred to me in time! "Thou shalt not tempt the Lord." Now I can shirk that dangerous leap, and no one can prove to me that I have flinched in the name of the divine majesty. I have covered myself very well by this text. Oh, yes; I can equal the devil in craftiness. I, too, can make well-calculated and well-timed use of the Bible to help me on the battlefield.' A fine fencing-match this, with nothing but the words of God for weapons!

But if it were so, why should Jesus be able to use the word-weapon and the word-thrust more effectively and with greater justice than the devil?

The word of God with which Jesus opposes the devil has higher authority solely and exclusively because for him, for Jesus, it represents the authority beneath which he stands. The word of God is only God's word and only his authority, as long as we ourselves humbly and obediently stand beneath it, as 'prisoners' of Jesus Christ (Eph. 3.1). If we 'exploit' it, if for

ulterior motives we say 'Lord, Lord' (Matt. 7.21ff), then instead
of being the word of God this word becomes a word of the
Accuser. That is why Jesus says to the people (Luke 6.46), 'Why
call ye me Lord, Lord, and do not the things that I say?' That
means: You do indeed use pious words; you turn your eyes up
to heaven, and seem to be on intimate terms with God; you
talk the language of Canaan; you say 'Lord, Lord' and 'God
says'; and yet all this is lies and a mean device of Satan. For
you do not have the slightest idea what that word means, and
thus you deprive it of all authority.

Thus it comes about that the frivolous and unauthorised use
of God's promise to send his helping angels becomes in the
mouth of the tempter really and truly a word of the devil. And
so it was and still is. Newspapers, books, partisan pamphlets
issued by the enemies of God—naturally take their stand on the
fact of God. Naturally they have 'religion deep in them'—these
newspapers, books and pamphlets are full to overflowing with
quotations from scripture plucked out of their context and dis-
torted into a hellish grimace. It is not God, but the Ape of God
that speaks here—with words borrowed from the Lord himself.

The Ape of God always uses the same tricks, and only changes
the shape in which he meets us. Sometimes he comes like a
preacher with unctuous, seductive voice; sometimes he mas-
querades as a mighty hero; sometimes he appears erect and
imposing like the statue of a reformer and religious liberator.
How humbly he can say 'Lord, Lord'; how illuminating do his
words sound: 'Lo, here is the Christ, there is the Christ'! How
well his Bible texts relieve our anxiety; how pleasantly his har-
monium makes music, how thunderously his giant-organ peals
in worship!

But we know now why these words become words of the
tempter, why they have no authority. We know now why Jesus
alone has the power, the shattering power to say: 'Again it is
written—this alone and nothing else.'

32. *Powers and Slaves*

Jesus bears this text aloft in his battle against the devil like
a commanding, annihilating banner. This banner he follows
blindly, and in its sign he wins the fight. But while this banner
of victory flies solitary over the battlefield, we see simultaneously

the ultimate strategic framework within which the whole event takes place. It concerns more than just the destiny to be decided between the demonic power (and therefore between the highest reality next to God) and man, in this case the man Jesus. On the contrary the principals in this fight are God and the Evil One—good and evil. And man is placed in the middle of this conflict and becomes the slave and ally of one or other of the combatants. We are an instrument played upon either by God or the Evil One. We are soldiers under the orders either of God or of the Evil One. We are all of us (the writer and the reader of this book alike) on the pay-roll of the one or the other (Rom. 6.16ff). Each of us has a treasure on which his heart is set; and it is his lord, the axis on which his life turns. And this treasure is either God or the Evil One (Matt. 6.19ff). We cannot free ourselves from this Either-Or through our works or through our achievements. We have seen how all this, too, may secretly (deep in our hearts) be accomplished against God and for our own glory, thus placing us on the pay-roll of the Evil One. Neither are we freed from this Either-Or by the apparently innocent, and yet so naïvely cunning thought: 'Do you mean that we are someone's slaves and always in subjection to someone other than ourselves?' we ask with the ingenuous rhetoric of astonished simplicity, the underlying assumption being that we are free agents. Our naïveté can only laugh, bitterly or humorously, at the idea of such a subordination, and it begins to remember with pride man's two legs and his head which towers above his body and can touch the stars, like the head of a titan.

Yes; we always belong to a lord, and are always borne upon a wave which may be in the ocean of God or the ocean of the Evil One. Indeed it often happens that even 'natural man' feels this fact for a moment, although he does not know whence the fact comes or whither it is tending. Occasionally he sees how the individual man has his opinion whispered into his ear by the spirit of the age, or by the masses, and how he (who is otherwise a quiet, thoughtful, steady man on whose judgment one can depend) is thrust into a mob and roused by its dynamic force to scream with it today 'Hosanna' and tomorrow 'Crucify', while later, at home in his private room, he regards himself with bewilderment in the mirror: Was it I who shouted that,

I, Jack Wilson? Yes, I suppose I did it because everyone was shouting above me, round me, through me; my nerves were electrically charged; the atmosphere was glowing; the screams and shouts seemed to go right through me, and I suppose my voice just joined in.

The man of this world talks of 'mass-suggestion' in such circumstances, without indeed knowing what he means by it. But this means—considered in the light of our story and its Either-Or—nothing else but that surrounding man there are fascinating and insidious whispers of persuasion or suggestion, which lead him like a dominating voice, just as wireless beams can steer ships or rockets or aeroplanes. Thus it came about that man did what this fascinating voice wished. So he shouted 'Crucify'. He did this in the belief that it was he himself who shouted, and that he personally had taken the decision, and wished to shout. And yet he shouted to order. He was under the spell of invisible spirits in the air; he was a slave to some lord—what lord? Would not the magnetic needle, if it possessed a mind, think, asked Leibniz, that its own will and decision pointed it to the north? Would not guided missiles, if they had human heads, maintain that they made their manoeuvres of their own free will, and by their own actions? And yet at the controls would sit a master whom they did not know, whose existence they did not even suspect. And meanwhile they would fly merrily and rejoice to find how easily steered and manoeuvred they were.

33. *Technology as Tool and as 'Power'*

There are yet other phenomena from which even 'natural man' may deduce some idea concerning the fact that we are ridden when we believe we are riders. Is not technology such a rider? Obviously it is put into our hands that we may rule the earth with it (Gen. 1.26ff). God gave it as a means into our hand. But did not the dynamite that lies hidden in that means—or in the man that uses it?—explode for the first time during the building of the Tower of Babel? Is it not a dynamite that explodes as soon as it meets the spark of human ambition and its titanic hybris? For technology is a thing which can raise those who use it to greatness and power over the masses, which can even become for a man a citadel against God. And as soon as the responsible engineer 'Man' allows all this to happen to him, or rather as soon as he does this 'with the help' of technology (for technology is not an evil in itself), he surrenders to the Evil One, and puts both himself and his technical means into Satan's hand.

Has not something like this happened in the case of humanity? Who would dare to say today that technology, that means of human power, really remains a means which man holds in his hands and has at his disposal? Who is not forced to acknowledge, even if unwillingly and with shuddering horror, that today, in our century, it is exactly the other way round—that technology possesses man, that it has, as it were, revolted and broken loose, and is no longer a power in man's hand but rather a power over man? Did it not inspire the decisive political and economic movements of the nineteenth century? (Here we will invoke only the catchword 'Capitalism' as a symptom of these events.) Would the emergence of 'the masses' as a 'fourth estate', even be conceivable without the industrialisation which is itself conditioned by technology? Would Marxism, above all in its Bolshevik form, be conceivable without the emergence of such a 'fourth estate'? And again, would a single one of our contemporary world-harassing, ideological forces be conceivable without the demonic storm-centre of Bolshevism, even though, indeed precisely because, these powers 'know' themselves called to oppose it; even though, indeed precisely because, they only wish to return an answer to it—a negative answer, but one which is forced from them none the less, and the tendency of which is determined in no small degree by the adversary himself?

In the last resort technology is one of the decisive factors which dictate to our century how it is to act. It would be foolish to decry technology itself as 'good' or 'evil' on the basis of these instances. And even the most powerful 'miracle-men', as Luther calls them, when seen in this light, appear only as men floating on this wave, called to the scene by an emergency at sea (and indeed by many other similar distresses!) and knocking together a few boats.

Seen from this angle, it is a merciful but dangerous illusion that 'men make history'. Far from it! We are all afloat in the same ship, and none of us can disembark. The ship has a captain and officers who steer it over the waves of this tumultuous age,

foaming and shaken to its uttermost depths. That is their sole
distinction from the rest. All else is illusion and a dream born
of fear. For the sea dictates their actions, and the sea rages
according to laws over which we have no control. And one of
these laws (not the Supreme Law, of course, but a law which
illustrates this phenomenon)—one of these laws is technology,
that technology which has gone wild and slipped out of man's
hand, and is now in process of exploding, so that he must seek
shelter from it, while still endeavouring to get the best results
from its unleashed power.

We are not trying to construct an interpretation of history
from all this. Only here does it seem to become perfectly clear
that man always belongs to someone, that he is the subordinate,
that he is never the lord of the sea, but at best an impressive
swimmer in its waves.

But that is saying little indeed. It is more important to iden-
tify the power in whose service we stand. And our text speaks
of this. It says there are two lords and we can be the servant of
either. One we shall love, the other we shall hate (Matt. 6.24).
We must fall into the hands of one or other of them, so that we
shall be either servants of the Evil One or children of the Father
who saves us. We may well ask in whose service we stand. Into
whose service are we led by means of those powers on which we
float, and which possess us already here below? Under what
symbol does all this happen, to whom does all this 'belong', to
which of the two? But who could answer this question? And
who would be allowed to answer it except by the prayer: 'Thy
kingdom come . . . deliver us from the Evil One'?

The issue lies in this play of forces. And indeed it is more than
a play of forces; it is God's fight for our soul; it is his violent
knocking at the locked door of our heart—that door which was
locked by another (Luke 12.36; Rev. 3.20). It is the rising of
his light over the darkness, whose secret ruler fights against the
light, and does not allow it to be comprehended (John 1.5).

It is good for once to understand God's fight for the world as
a battle of powers, and not always to oversimplify matters and
look upon man as the fighter, and therefore as the ostensible
centre of events. We must be quite clear about this if we want
to understand the background of this conflict in the desert. We
are so enlightened, so possessed by the thought that we are the

measure of all things and the central theme of world-history—and therefore also by the thought that we are the combatants fighting for God—that we cannot understand this background by ourselves.

The issue likewise is decided at a place—and by this the background is indicated—where it is not we who fight, but where others fight over us, so much so that God can bleed for us, and hangs on the cross on our behalf. In the Communion service this blood and this death are commemorated as a sign of communion with him; as a sign that we are his and are torn free from all other feudal duty; as a sign that God is for us and that therefore no power in heaven or earth or hell can be against us or can separate us from God (Rom. 8.31ff). That is the ultimate strategic framework of this event. That is the fight between God and the tempter for our soul.

But we know who has always won in this fight. We know who will win in this forsaken hour. We know it, even though we walk through this world as men who are fought over and raged over and tempted and frightened, until we see God in his glory face to face. We know it, even when we have become casualties in the struggle which is ordained for us in our hearts or in the world outside or in ecclesiastical history, and refuse to believe that we are in the victor's army and that the victory is already won in that fight which we are still fighting. That is the joyful news amid the terrors of the End, and that is the divine refreshment which strengthens us against the hoof-beats of the apocalyptic horsemen.

And now let us look upon the victor in this fight in the decisive moment of his victory—the third and last stage. But we already know that he who gains the prize in the end shall be the victor. And that victor is Jesus Christ.

THE THIRD TEMPTATION:
JESUS' KINGDOM OF THIS WORLD

Again, the devil taketh him up to a very high mountain, and pointeth out to him all the kingdoms of the world and the glory of them, and saith to him, All these things I will give thee, if, falling down, thou shalt adore me. Then Jesus saith to him, Depart, Satan; for it is written, Thou shalt adore the Lord thy God, and him alone thou shalt worship.

34. *The Shining Landscape*

THE tempter advances to the last attack. Royal crowns glitter; states stand ready to abandon their gods and idols and accept Christ as their lord. 'The world for Jesus Christ!' sounds hopefully in Jesus' ears. He hears a rustling as of many, many flags. An opportunity of sublime power! He is not to win the earth painfully and be kept constantly struggling for it; he will not have to weep continually over Jerusalem (Luke 19.41); he will not have to be crucified continually; the darkness will not always fail to comprehend him (John 1.5); he will not always feel his breast torn with the sorrow of God—sorrow for this world: No, here comes the world itself, here he sees it lying bright before him, offered to his hand: Jerusalem, the city of sorrow; the mighty Roman Empire, already on the verge of decay; the youthful Britannia, and the infinitely many other villages, towns and lands. They all fling open their gates, and this opening seems to be accompanied by distant singing: 'Thy king cometh!' And he, no one but he, Christ, is to be this King. And the gates of the world are wide open for the movement which he is to kindle on the earth, and which will be called Christianity. People will never fall away from Christianity again; everything which fills this earth in space and time will belong to him: 'Thy king cometh!'

But is not this song a parody? A parody of a song which comes to him out of his own future: 'Thy king cometh!' There they are in truth singing about his kingship, and strewing palms and shouting joyful ovations; they are beside themselves with

63

intoxicating homage. Is not this the fulfilment of what the devil promises him here—the jubilant fulfilment of his royal kingship, and his enthronement as lord of this earth?

No, it is the way to the cross! It is the way to the ruin of the kingdom, or to the ironical kingship, the charter of which hangs as a scrap of paper on his cross (Matt. 27.37): 'This is the King of the Jews.' Then the bawling mob will shout jubilantly for Barabbas, and not for him (Matt. 27.16). Which of these two now is the real kingship, and which the parody? Is the kingship on the cross the parody of this real, indubitable, public kingship which is being offered him here in the desert, or—is it the other way round?

35. *The Globe in the Devil's Hand*

But then the scales fall from his eyes, and shuddering he realises that the earth which is being offered to him is a globe in the hand of the devil, who turns it seductively and makes it glitter in front of him. The only earth offered to him is this globe. And the face of the seducer smiles behind the little sphere, behind the toy which is so lovely to look at and so exciting, because it brings with it such power (Gen. 3.6). The seducer knows that 'knowledge' and 'power' are tremendous attractions!

All that can be so vividly imagined is clearly implicit in the neat little phrase with which the seducer rounds off his offer, which can be overlooked almost as easily as the ending 'yours faithfully' or 'all best wishes'. It looks as if the seducer had already turned away from Jesus to look—himself quite fascinated—into the shining landscape, and were now turning again, for the last time, to nod to Jesus and whisper casually: 'Of course, only if you fall down and worship me!'

Then, presumably, he turns away again, doing his best to appear indifferent, hoping that Jesus has not heard his last remark and has failed to notice his cloven hoof. For the devil knows that one must give men the chance of missing something, that one must lead them to sin over golden bridges which soothe their scruples. He knows that it would be foolish to say: 'Listen, you Son of God; I want to subject you to myself. Sign your name first in your blood. Then I'll compensate you in one way or another.' No, it cannot be done as simply as that! The conscience of the son of God—as of the sons of men—must be treated cautiously and tactically. Conscience must be given the chance to overlook or fail to hear something. What one really wants—thinks the devil—must be whispered, while one looks the other way. Jesus sees through this at once, and notices that the subordinate clause: 'If thou wilt fall down and worship me' is properly the principal clause, and that this is the card on which the seducer has staked everything.

But afterwards the seducer, sitting alone among the ruins of his hopes, thinks: 'What didn't succeed with the Lord, may still come off with the servants. I'll keep on repeating the same experiment with the church of this Christ, anyhow. "Christianity" will remain my deadly enemy. But I won't be such a fool as to tell Christianity so. No, for if I do, this Christianity will become very sharp of hearing, its conscience will awaken, and it will feel called to the *status confessionis. Status confessionis* denotes a situation or state in which one must confess fully and freely. This *status* I hate more than all the holy-water-basins and incense-smoke in the world. When men have yielded to it, one can do no more with them—absolutely nothing more. Then they let themselves be burnt, torn in pieces, eaten by lions, crucified, slaughtered, hanged—anything rather than fall down and worship me. No, the *status confessionis* I must avoid, at all costs!

'How shall I do it? There are diabolically simple recipes for that. All I need to do is to give the sons of God and men, the churches and Christian religions, the chance to overlook or fail to realise the fact that they are in the *status confessionis*; everything concerned with that must be hidden away in subordinate clauses, put at the tail end of the sentence or left between the lines, and afterwards I must spring upon them the fact that they have incidentally signed themselves over to me.'

36. *Jesus' Vision on the Exceeding High Mountain*

Does the devil often have cause to complain that his tactics fail abysmally though never again so appallingly as here in the desert?

Does he often have to remind himself that he has to deal not only with Christians, but with the living God? Will he succeed with his subordinate clauses, his tail ends of sentences and his efforts at camouflage?

'. . . if thou wilt fall down and worship me.' He let that small subordinate clause slip out as if by accident. And yet it is the secret condition behind everything:

'Thou canst have bread, thou Son of God—if thou wilt fall down and worship me.'

'Thou canst proclaim thyself to the world by a miracle, and leap from the pinnacles of the temple—if thou wilt fall down and worship me.'

'Thou canst have all the kingdoms of the world and their glory—if thou wilt fall down and worship me.'

What can have passed through Jesus' soul during all this?

Not that we have the right to plumb this secret, nor may we consider this as a fitting object of our inquisitiveness. But we may assess the possibilities which offered themselves to his eyes, and shudder for a moment at the prospects which were revealed to them.

There he stood on an exceeding high mountain and saw his disciples from all the ages, who acclaimed him: 'This Jesus (that is I, who stand up here) must speak the decisive word of redemption for the world.' And now he saw that these disciples wished to force hardened mankind to hear this word, and that they wished to use violence to help his teaching to victory. The princes and the unknown soldiers of the church wanted to make his name into a banner of violence, into a holy flag to be borne in their vanguard and beneath which they would die—in a thousand great and small crusades and retreats from crusades. Could he not have had all that here—and much more cheaply —if he had not been compelled to reject it? Would men understand this refusal? Or, would even those who had seen the light condemn so extraordinary a rejection?

He saw cultures and centuries bearing his name. He saw 'Christian' states.

He, who knew not, and would never know, where he should lay his head (Matt. 8.20), and who suffered hunger and thirst in a lonely desert, saw pomp and circumstance displayed in his name.

All this he saw—and behind it the cross as the other possibility. Were not the countries of the world a bemusing, an intoxicating possibility? Could he not utilise them for his task, for his sacred goal? Why must acceptance of this offer necessarily mean betraying his task? Certainly, his kingdom was not of this world; but would it not be a good thing to subject this earth to that coming Age?

All this Jesus may have considered in this moment. It was the moment in which he seemed to stand at the zenith of his life.

Was he not on an exceeding high mountain—where would he be in the next moment—where—down there? Which of the many kings and procurators down there, now ready to kiss his feet at the slightest encouragement, will persecute him and torment him—and crucify him?

All these lands and kingdoms, with the glory of their cities and the splendour of their princes, Jesus saw.

And he saw, too, the other side of the picture, the darkness of his own future, and questions formed themselves in his mind.

Why must God always be so defenceless in this world? Was he not the Lord? Why were people allowed to blaspheme him and spit in his Son's face?

Could not the movement which he was to kindle on earth, could not 'Christianity' be a world-view, a mythos, capable of holding together whole peoples, cultures and centuries?

Was he himself to be no more than a ferment of dissolution on this earth, a stone of stumbling (Isa. 8.14) and rock of offence (Rom. 9.33; 1 Cor. 1.23; Gal. 5.11), upon which opinions would only divide and diverge—as a pier in a bridge divides the stream which surges against it?

And if Jesus himself did not think this, his disciples from all ages and peoples have struggled with the thought, and wrestle with the shimmering vista which they saw from the top of the mountain on which they stood, and to which they were ever being led anew. Certainly this Jesus had come to cast fire upon the earth (Luke 12.49). But was not this fire too weak to lay the earth in ashes and so hasten the coming of the new world? And was it not too strong to be stifled? And was it not for this reason a focus of unrest, a flickering, irritating flame, harassing men and hurting them?

So thought and think Christians even today when, following their Master, they are led up to the 'high mountain' and quarrel with God.

37. *The Faintheartedness of Christians*

Jesus saw all this. He saw how things would go. He saw how men despaired over his defencelessness, his lowliness and his far from kingly 'look of a servant': 'How long will you keep our souls in suspense? If you are the Christ, then tell us so frankly (John 10.24); tell us so openly, mightily, impressively and without ambiguity'—thus men cried.

'Art thou he that cometh, or is he for whom we wait another?' (Matt. 11.3) thus they wrangled and waited for a new banner which would be openly and splendidly unfurled, and for which they would gladly die.

He saw—and what a contrast it was to the shining kingdoms down there!—the little groups of two or three (Matt. 18.20) fainthearted and tempted in their helplessness. Would they still be able to believe that all things come from God, belong to God and are done through God's agency (Rom. 11.36), when they saw so little evidence of him and his Son? He saw the disciples as on his departure he vanished from their eyes, and left them alone (Luke 24.51; Acts 1.9).

He heard his own cry: 'Eloi, Eloi, lama sabachthani', that is, 'My God, my God, why hast thou forsaken me?' (Mark 15.34).

Why must he plunge the world in unrest and yet be so powerless? Why must he cause such unrest through his weakness—by the mystery of the weakness of God?

No doubt it was true that the men of this world are rebels and revolutionaries, that they are impious in their hearts, worship gods of their own, and do not seek for the real God. But would it not be better and more merciful if God kept this secret to himself, instead of shouting it aloud to the world through his Son, and through his apostles and prophets, and then keeping this awesome silence and waiting for men? And—if he must shout it—why only from the cross and not rather with thunderous, resounding, heavenly voice, accompanied by sword and power and dominion, so that men must hear this secret for very mercy's sake?

It was indeed hard to be merely a man who was crucified. Yes, it was hard to be only a stone dropped into the pool of this world, to make its circles evermore, while itself vanishing from sight.

The devil whispers all this to the Son of God, with words, gestures, and a show of splendour. Then he turns away again. For one must allow time for what one has said and demonstrated to take effect. One must leave men to the tumult in their soul. The tempter knows that his best fulcrum is in men's souls.

38. *The Clash of the Tempter with God*

But now Jesus answers—and his answer makes the devil whip round. And like all the other answers, this answer results from the fact that Jesus Christ retreats from the centre of the conflict, and goes behind God. For he knows that it is God about whom and against whom the fight is waged. Thus Jesus indicates the main lines of this event by stepping back behind God. He places this struggle in the one perspective from which it can be seen, and from which the conflicting powers can be clearly identified. Jesus steps back behind God, exactly as he did earlier, by stepping under his word: 'It is written'. And this word says: 'Thou shalt worship the Lord, thy God, and him only shalt thou serve' (Matt. 4.10).

The Lord is here called into the arena. Does the devil know what that means? Does he suspect now in what he has become involved? Does he suspect what it means to attack Christ, in whose person God himself opposes him and smites him with his sword? And does he suspect what it means to persecute the church of Christ which is his body (1 Cor. 10.16; 12.27; Eph. 1.23); and to lay hands on God's people, whom he guards like the apple of his eye (Deut. 32.10), and to oppress the disciples of Christ, who, having died with him (Rom. 6.8), are lost to themselves and to sin (Rom. 6.11; Gal. 2.19; Col. 3.3), and now live only in him (Rom. 8.1; 2 Cor. 5.17; Phil. 1.21), and Christ in them (Gal. 2.20)? Does he suspect whom he has challenged, and that it is not flesh and blood that is raised against him like a mighty arm (Isa. 52.10; Jer. 17.5) to strike him down from the mountain, down into his gloomy valleys and abysses: 'Get thee hence, Satan'? Does he suspect that he is recognised when he breaks into the midst of the temple—that he is recognised even when he succeeds by means of an impudently daring trick in making apostles, bishops and superintendents file in solemn procession before him? How the words thunder against him, 'Get behind me, Satan! You are a hindrance to me. For you are not on the side of God, but of men' (Matt. 16.23).

Yes; the tempter may suspect that his thrust was not into flesh, but has found the living God, the Lord himself. He has heard the words—and had to tremble at them—proclaiming that the Son of God became man, that he was tempted just as we are, and that all that happens to those who are his, happens to him. 'Whoso toucheth you, toucheth the apple of mine eye' (Zech. 2.8). The framework of this event becomes plain here. The framework is God and Satan, with man as the sword of the one or the other—the apple of the eye of one or the other, but with God, not himself, as the central theme.

39. *The Mystery of the Defencelessness of Jesus*

What does all this mean? Surely this:

God became man in Jesus Christ, was oppressed by the Evil One in our stead, and in company with us as our brother and companion. Stated in the dry words of dogma, that is the immediate explanation of why God seems so defenceless in this world, why on the cross he submits himself so defencelessly and uncomplainingly to his enemies, and lets them spit upon him and kill him. That is the explanation of why Jesus *must* here despise powers and kingdoms, why he remains poor and weaponless and submits to men. His defencelessness belongs to the inmost essence of his calling.

His calling consists in proclaiming the love of God, in his bringing with him the love of God, in its being incarnate in him: 'God so loved the world, that he gave his only-begotten Son . . .' (John 3.16). And this love is so incomprehensible in its wonder because it says:

Look, there is God at your side as your brother, become a man like you. And he who walks there on your right, O man, is the God whom you deny in all your works, ways and thoughts, without whom you desire to live, and from whom you desire to be free and safe, above all because you are afraid of him. You are like those who say: 'Stop thief!' for you say: 'God is dead', and fail to realise that you yourself are dead, that you died long ago in the sight of God, and you are stagnating, as your gods do (despite all the activity of your life). Do you appeal to your greatness and splendour and power, O man? Ah, are not your gods and ideologies mighty and imposing, full of wealth and

skill and lofty thought, and yet they are as dead when you look
upon the Living One—and are as nothing when you look at
him who is all things—are annihilated when you come to know
him you called 'those things which be not as though they were'
(Rom. 4.17; Rev. 1.8)? So you yourself are dead, O man, before
the Living God, you and your gods. You are dead before the
Living God.

And do you know what this death of yours consists in? It
consists in your having no communion with God and your being
troubled by the wrath of the Living One (Ps. 90.7), since he
knows you. And therefore everything that comes from God
must be a new death to you (Rom. 7.10, 13). You must die
because of God again and again, as men and creatures must
die who come into the orbit of his majesty and touch the holy
mount (Exod. 19.12): that is your sickness unto death. And
being dead means here that God removes himself infinitely far
from you, as indeed you have deserved that he should; it means
that he flees beyond the horizon of your life and you no longer
have any communion with him, and wander round lost. To
pursue your own religion, O man, and study the consolations
of your worldly wisdom, means only an endless wandering.

And look, now this distant God has come near to you in
incomprehensible love. When you could not take hold of him,
he has taken hold of you. When you could not seek him, he
found you. When you were persecuting him, he loved you.

You ask how that came about? It happened thus—God came
down to you and searched for you. It happened thus—he became your brother. It happened thus—he planted himself in
the abyss which yawned between you and him, which you had
torn open in defiance. It happened thus—he placed himself
in the same rank as you, he was found to be in the likeness of
man (Phil. 2.7), he is tempted just as you and I (Heb. 4.15),
and endures the Evil One with you, and at your side. It happened thus—he takes your loneliness upon his shoulders (Mark
15.34), dies your death, tastes your fear (Mark 14.33), has endured captivity (Luke 22.47ff) and taken it captive (Eph. 4.8).

Do you see now what God's defencelessness in this world
means? Do you see that it is the sign of his love, his brotherhood with you, the sign of his becoming man? Do you realise
that the sacrifice which is proclaimed here is a sacrifice of God?

F

He hands himself over to you; and the cross shows what you do with him. But is not the cross therefore—in spite of all—the greatest token of his love? Does it not stand at the end of the path of his love towards you? And is it not also still love, defenceless love, that in the cross he reveals how you regard him in your deepest heart—namely rejecting, failing to comprehend and return his love—and how, in a last demonstration of his unchanging love, and your unchanging hate, he dies on your account?[1] God must die on man's account so that man may learn his heart, and that he may see tested and unveiled those things which he does not know about himself or only dimly suspects (Ps. 139.23f; 1 Cor. 13.12). God must die for man, so that man may simultaneously—and transcending all this—know the heart of God and be allowed to understand that it is completely opened to him, and is full of Good News. That is the mystery of the defencelessness of God.

40. *Grace and Judgment in Jesus' Defencelessness*

This mystery can only be paraphrased in a new mystery, the mysterious word 'grace'. It is grace when God, the distant God, comes to man, gives himself to him and thus endures being surrendered to him. It is grace when he sometimes throws off this concealment and his disguise as the brother, the servant, the crucified, the tempted, the defenceless one, and even in the beggar's dress and in the shadow of the cross becomes visible as the Lord of lords and King of kings (Matt. 16.16). God is openly, bodily, present in the Word become flesh—in Christ. That is grace. But it is again grace when he reveals himself to us—to you and me—and is not confused with beggars and founders of religions, as our silly, limited eyes would like to confuse him. It is all grace: that Christ is there, and that he is there for us; that the light came into the darkness, and that it came to us and to me—how else could we have known it?

---

[1] The Passiontide hymns of the church know how to sing that the Son of God dies in me—must die in me—and that herein my heart is laid bare in a terrible way which is endurable only because Golgotha is at the same time the incomprehensible sign of forgiveness: 'Now what Thou, Lord, endurest, / Is all my burden; / I myself brought upon myself, / What Thou hast borne. / Look hither, here I stand wretched, / Having deserved wrath. / Give me, O Pitier, / The sight of Thy mercy.' — 'I—I and my sins . . . they have caused the misery which befalls Thee, and the mournful army of martyrs' (P. Gerhardt) — 'Even though my guilt / Caused Thee to endure, my Saviour, / Such torment and distress, / In bitter death on the cross.'

Luther knew this and witnessed to it again and again; God's grace is defencelessness, and not power; it is the cross, and not the glory; it is the still small voice, and not fire or earthquake (1 Kings 19.11ff); it is to be 'believed', and not to be 'seen', it is a gift of the Spirit, not an open demonstration (John 20.24-9).

God's grace with its mystery is all this. And its deepest mystery is that it is always, at the same time, judgment, that it always has this other, darker side: for is it not terrifyingly true that one can hide from this grace, that (just because it is defenceless) one may blaspheme against it and reject it, while we cannot treat the secular power in this way? May we not speak with impunity of the 'imaginary Lord'? May we not with impunity misuse this defenceless grace and the defenceless Lord for any and every purpose—for perjury, for cunning religious policy, for golden ornaments, for giving pious thrills—or for a scapegoat, upon whose back we can unload the alleged maldevelopment of our people or indeed of occidental history? And no lightning strikes. No, the lamb goes to the slaughter (Isa. 53.7) ever anew, ever anew—and nothing happens to its tormentors, as far as we can see.

The grace of God is a question put to the world, and the world (which is we who write and read here) now has the answer. And then comes the day of God—and then the questions are over, then God alone, and only he, is the answerer. And his answer is shield and sword, fire and power, earthquake and storm. The defenceless one is proclaimed to all the world as the Almighty, as he who was always this Almighty. He who dwelt among us without a kingdom and without the splendour of this world, yet bore this earth in his hand. He who was poorer and more homeless than the foxes was yet the Lord of all creatures. 'I (the Almighty) was hungry and ye gave me no meat. I (the Almighty) was thirsty and ye gave me no drink. I (the Almighty) was a stranger, and ye took me not in. I (the Almighty) was naked, and ye clothed me not. (I the Almighty) was sick and in prison—was defenceless—and ye visited me not' (Matt. 25.42ff).

Then they will ask: Where wast thou then? We did not see thee! We saw only cross and lowliness, where we expected glory. Where were thy credentials? Who could have told us it was thou? There are so many lying prophets and pseudo-kings!

Then the Lord will point to the long train of his servants, the persecuted, the naked, the destitute, the hungry and thirsty, the crucified, the burned, who belonged to his body, in whom one touched the apple of his eye, and in whom one tormented and crucified and scorned himself.

And now comes the answer: 'Verily I say unto you, Inasmuch as ye did it not to one of the least of these, ye did it not unto me' (Matt. 25.45).

So all the defencelessness of God's Son and his grace is a prophecy for his day, for the open Lordship of God, which here has only begun, and is only secretly present, while he waits at the back door of the world as a scorned Lazarus, because the rich lord in the house does not want him to pass his threshold. It waits and trembles in secret power; for all belongs to it. It has trickled already through the framework of the house; and a tremor as of abysmal powers shakes the pillars and façades again and again. But the rich man thinks that it is the stamping of his mighty foot that does this. And he lays costly carpets on the stone, so that the growling of the depths no longer disturbs him.

EPILOGUE

WHEN Jesus had said all this and performed all this against the devil, 'then the devil leaveth him, and lo, angels approached, and waited on him'.

What a conclusion to this hour! And what abysses and heavenly kingdoms are included in this hour! Christ was 'tempted like as we are'—that is one marvel of this hour. For because he was so tempted he has 'compassion with our weakness', and we have a brother in the profoundest danger in our life. There is now no longer any lonely point in this life.

Yet there lies another marvel in all this: 'He was tempted like as we are—but without sin'.

Can we fathom what that means?

We think of our starting-point; we think how Jesus had to go into the desert, into solitude, to be tempted, and not—as seemed obvious—into the world of sinful, seductive opportunities. That was a hint to us of the meaning of temptation. For we saw that the secret of temptation is the temptability of man. This secret lies in man himself, not outside him, not for instance in his opportunities for sinning. In him yawns the abyss, even if he leaps over it a thousand times. He is tempted by theft because he is a thief, even though in fact he does not steal. He is tempted to kill because he is a murderer, even though in fact he does not slay his brother.

So the possibility of our being tempted to lie, to thieve, to be adulterous, proves us to be lying creatures. We cannot change this fundamental constitution of our life, even if we fight for truth and against lies with every nerve of our body and soul. The temptation to lie remains; the abyss yawns within us; sin lies in wait in implacable desire. That is the awe-inspiring lesson of the temptation. 'Wretched man that I am! Who shall deliver me from the body of this death?' (Rom. 7.24).

Here becomes plain the last and most profound marvel of Jesus' temptation, the incomprehensible marvel that we must worship: that he was tempted without sin. This is the marvel

75

that raises him above us and does not allow his being to be exhaustively defined by saying that he is simply the brother who shares our suffering. Because he is tempted as we are, he has probed our lowest depths. But because this temptation was not a sign that an abyss yawned within him, and that Satan lay hidden in him somehow already—because this temptation came upon him, the pure, the sinless one, and he passed through it, untouched, as later through the mob that wished to seize him; because of all this, he is the Lord over temptation, the royal victor.

Sinless and yet tempted—that is, as we see now, a riddle which our intellect will never grasp—a marvel before our eyes, a divine profundity, like all that meets us in Jesus.

So we see him, amidst his lowliness and brotherhood with man, highly exalted above all humanity, which is impure even in temptation. We see him exalted as the Lord who has trodden sin under his feet, as the high priest who is more than all priests of the race of man, in their fallenness into sin and death.

Thus we have a double consolation:

Because Christ is our brother, we are not alone in our temptation. He suffers it with us, down to the lowest depths which Satan has conceived.

And because he is the Lord, who stands in the purity of heaven beyond all sin, we may pray him to keep us from temptation. We are certain of his love to all eternity. Christ not only marches on our right hand against death and devil; but he upholds us, too, from his height, because he is the Lord.

The knowledge that we are sheltered by his power gives us that peace which the world cannot give or take away from us. How uncertain is the peace which the world gives! Perhaps it is the quiet achieved by those who believe they have unveiled the meaning of world history, and resign themselves to it in peace, because they have found a resting-point in the flux of outward appearances; or perhaps it is the uninterested indifference of those who take it as it comes. But the peace of Jesus, which the world cannot give or take away, is the peace of that double certainty that Christ is Lord of the events which surge about us—and is Lord, too, of that depth in the stream of human events which we found to be temptation, as hanging between God and Satan. And it is the peace given by the other

certainty, that even in that event, and even in those depths
Christ is with us.

Lord and brother, King and comrade, our ruler and the
sharer of our suffering; that is the sublime wonder of the saving
power of Jesus. We march beneath this wonder as beneath the
sky which arches over us, wherever we may stand. We live in
the name of this wonder. Jesus our Lord and brother! That is
what gives us the peace that is higher than all reasoning.

INDEX OF
PASSAGES OF SCRIPTURE

INDEX OF PASSAGES OF SCRIPTURE